On Copywriting: How To Make Money Writing

Joel Mark Harris

Table of Contents

Preface

I have always believed that writing advertisements is the second most profitable form of writing. The first, of course, is ransom notes.

-Philip Dusenberry

For many years, I thought I wanted to be J.D Salinger. My dad introduced the great writer to me at an early age. I remember he would out loud "A Perfect Day For Banana Fish" to me in his large bedroom overlooking 9th Avenue, not far from Trimble Park. His poetic voice slowly reading the words on the page, acting out the various characters. I can't think of a perfect story. It was sad and sweet and seemed to encompass life so expertly.

As a kid, I thought Salinger was the coolest – writing one classic book and then fading off into the darkness. People would camp outside of the post office in hopes to catch a glimpse of him. There seemed something alluring about it. Something sexy, something romantic.

Like a lot of teenagers – especially boys – I identified with Holden Caulfield's anti-establishment behavior. His loneliness, hopliness, and his feeling of isolation. His longing for a kinder, gentler world, where kids didn't have to grow up.

As a kid, I was a bit of a recluse. I didn't want to deal with society or the people in it. (I think that's how all writers grow up.) I was safe in my little bubble, reading in my bedroom. Not that society had been particularly cruel to me. I had an amazing childhood growing up, but there was this entire promotional aspect I wasn't too comfortable with. I felt marketing was dirty. I loved how Salinger could just put a book out there and with little effort, or so it seemed to me, make it an instant classic.

I remember just before I finished writing my first book, I had an argument with the co-producer of my movie about whether I should even have a website or not. Whether I should join Facebook or not. I didn't want to be that guy who flaunts his stuff all the time. I didn't want to be a salesman. Not only did I hate it, but I thought that the work spoke for itself. I was an artist. Marketing was a dirty word.

I worked for Starbucks for 15 years, and I thought one day I will be able to support myself full time as a writer. I worked and worked, dreaming of the day when I would be free. And then the day came and I felt just as unfulfilled. I could control own schedule, do whatever I wanted but still, I felt lost. Hadn't I achieved my goal? Sure I wasn't as famous or as rich as Salinger but I never cared for those things. The loneliness was slowly strangling me, making me feel empty. Questions like what was I doing with my life? Was I going down the right direction?

It wasn't until then I realized I could never handle being on my own. I had started my own marketing firm and it was then I truly realized that this romantic ideal was just that – an idealized version of life. It wasn't real.

J.D Salinger died in 2010 and with him, my feelings of trying to emulate him died as well. I didn't mourn him like I have done with my other favourite authors in the past, authors like Michael Crichton. Salinger was a relic from the past, a boyhood's dream that you could write one successful novel that would change the world.

Somewhere along the way, I had become a different person or just realized that the thing I had been chasing my entire life was a fool's errand. Now it's my job to sell things. That's all copywriting is after all – using written words to sell products and services. In many ways, I have become the anti-Holden Caulfield. I have become part of the establishment, a part of the rat race. I work for big corporations and small businesses. I'm a gun for hire. Sure, I enjoy my art but even with it, I see that there is an art to selling. Even artists need to make a buck. I have become everything Caulfield would have despised. Am I okay with that? I can answer that with a resounding yes. Sure, sometimes, generally while I commute into the office I mourn the old me. The one who didn't want a website because it was too commercial. But would I go back to being that guy? I much prefer the worldly man I have become. The one who understands you can't just build it and expect people to come.

I have heard a rumor that Salinger wrote a sequel to Catcher In The Rye. I don't know if it's true or not, but I would have liked to think Holden Caulfield grew up too.

Introduction

Let us prove to the world that good taste, good art, and good writing can be good selling. –
William Bernbach

Recently I was walking down the street when one of those pushy charity people stopped me. You know the ones who seem a little too cheerful, a little too full of life. He was this long-haired hippy dude with bad teeth and he smelt funny. He told me that his name was Joel and we bonded over having the same name. He asked me what I did and I told him I was a copywriter.

"Like Don Draper?" he asked.

I wish, was my first thought. I think most guys wish they were at least half Don Draper. I, for one, don't dress up in expensive suits, or work at a swanky Manhattan office where we get drunk by 9 am. I live a very simple, quiet life in Vancouver, doing most of my work in a shared co-working space. I don't have a pretty secretary. I don't have a view of anything. In fact, my job isn't glamorous at all.

It got me thinking about how copywriting has changed so much since the age of Mad Men and turned into the age of WeWork. The tools of the trade are different, but the fundamentals of writing, advertisement, and selling haven't. Copywriting may seem old-fashioned, something from the Mad Men era, but it's more important than ever what with websites and social media and email. It seems people rarely respect the craft anymore, especially those outside of the marketing business.

No matter what somebody tells you, we communicate with words, both written and verbal. Whether it's with a friend, a family member, or a customer. To acquire a customer usually requires some sort of copywriting, whether you realize it or not.

The written word is more important now than ever before in this competitive market. Your headline, your text, and especially your emails can make or break your sales and can either increase your profits or send your business into a nosedive.

If you want to learn about how stellar copywriting can improve your business, increase leads, and double your sales then this is the book for you. But this book is more than about increasing your business. It's a book about life as a writer. I always wanted to be a writer ever since I could remember. In fact, I always had three career goals.

I could be an F-16 fighter pilot. (Not really a good career aspiration since the Canadian air force doesn't have any. The second was a soccer player. However, I didn't really have the speed or talent to make it anywhere. (Again, the Canadian thing made it difficult to compete with the top countries. We don't have the system to thrive in.)

The last thing was to be a writer. And since the fighter jet pilot and soccer star things didn't work out so well I decided to focus all my efforts on writing. Not that it's ever easy. For the longest time, I was a struggling copywriter. In fact, as I started school I lagged so far behind the other kids in the simple building blocks of learning. I remember having the distinct fear I would never learn how to read and write. Early on, I was diagnosed with mild learning disabilities. I was held back in second grade because I wasn't as fast as the other kids. Not a good start for a writer. Writing was always a struggle and it never came easy. Nothing ever was. But that's okay because I just worked harder than everybody else. It just took me a longer to get where most people were at, that's all.

I was never very good at school and always struggled through most subjects. I got extra time on all my tests and was put in special classes. All this demoralize my self-confidence more than did any good. It prevented me from taking risks or being able to do the things that needed to be done.

I don't know if it was the fact that it was tougher for me that made it even that more special or if it was just something naturally wanted to do. I never grew out of the bedtime story phase of my life.

Even after I became a successful, award-winning author of over six books, this fear never left me. It took me years to realize just how much the past was running my life. Even as wrote and produced a hugely successful independent film that was shown in over 30 festivals across the world.

Copywriting is special because it doesn't require flowery language or to even be a skilled writer. It's about being simple, direct and straightforward. It's not writing a bestselling novel, it is not creating a great screenplay, it's not about winning awards. It is about selling a product.

You do not need to use fancy language, big words, complex sentence structures. This might be a little bit controversial but it doesn't even matter if you spell your copy correctly. Don't let the grammar Nazis play mind tricks with you. (You can burn me at the stake later, if you must) It's about knowing the market and being able to understand sales and human psychology.

Will this book make you a million-dollar copywriter? I've got good and bad news for you on that front. You have all the tools for the trade. Everything to make you successful is already on the internet. There isn't anything intellectually I can tell you that will make much of a difference. There is no 'secret' or 'formula' or anything else that will suddenly make you a copywriting genius. There are no gurus or promises. No pixie dust to sprinkle on your keyboard. Sorry to burst your bubble.

However, if somebody like me can learn it then you can too! Let me assure you that, although it's easy, it doesn't mean there isn't work involved.

And now for the bad news. Not nearly enough companies value our services. Copywriting is the last thing on their mind. They think anybody can write good copy. I can't count the times I see fancy, well-designed websites with a poorly written copy. That's like going to a fancy restaurant and realizing they only serve hot dogs.

The techniques and strategies I teach in this book not only help me attract clients but also allows me to work on and pick the most interest projects. Not only have I worked for local companies but also expanded my reach into the United States, Britain and Switzerland. I worked with a corporate intelligence firm with a high-level FBI-security clearance. I have written copy for a top Manhattan law firm and a large Swiss Television Station, among others.

I can now work anywhere in the world with an internet connection! I am no longer tied to a desk or an office. If any of these things I mentioned appeal to you then keep on reading.

I will show you proven techniques that will get you high-paying clients right in your own city without spending tons of money on marketing or advertising.

The difference between a world-class copywriter and an okay copywriter that the okay copywriter sits down and only writes about the product. The world-class copywriter sits down, researches everything there is to know about the product and the ideal customer. The world-class copywriter speaks directly to his or her audience. Remember copywriting is sales in print. And sales is all about knowing your prospect.

It's crucial that when you're writing using words that people associate with something they want. This is the most powerful way to use words and marketing. If you're not offering people a way to make their lives better and find something else to do. You should always be offering value to your customers. The value of what you are offering should be incredibly obvious to you. But most people are skeptical first and they don't trust salespeople easily. You need to lay it out in real simple terms.

Although I often talk about freelancing in this book, most of the strategies and tactics can be used if you're working in as an employee too. And while I'm at it, a word of warning for all you employees out there. Just because you think you have a cushy job, doesn't mean you don't need to learn how to sell or learn how to pick up clients.

You should always strive to be what is known as a rainmaker – a person who brings in new accounts, adding value to the business. A rainmaker is confident, powerful and inspires a following. Being a rainmaker is the most important skill you can have. If you're a rainmaker, you will never be poor.

The origin of the rainmaker comes from the Native American practice of dancing to encourage rain to the necessary crops, often saving an entire village from starvation. The rainmaker was an honoured position in the tribe for his ability to support his fellow villagers.

My advice to you. Become a rainmaker. Then you don't need to worry about your job or where your next paycheque is coming from. You will be able to snap your fingers

Chapter One:

On How To Be a Top Copywriter

There is no such thing as an advertising genius

- Claude Hopkins

Let me ask you, why do you want to be a copywriter? Is it because you like writing and marketing? Or do you just want to make money writing? It's a difficult profession because most people don't recognize the value of good communication and writing. Clients tend to value good design over good writing. Design is flashy and sexy. Writing looks dull and limp on the page.

However, the good thing about being a writer is that it's very difficult to outsource. Almost everything else – coding, graphic designs, SEO, websites – can be outsourced to other countries. How many emails or calls do you get from India offering a new website or SEO services or some other marketing service. It's rare that you get somebody from India offering you writing. Right now, I'm employing developers in Ukraine, Serbia, Russia and India as well as Canada. Almost anything that isn't the English language can be created anywhere in the world. Just look at the Apple iPhone. It may be designed in the United States but every piece of it is built somewhere else in the world. It's so much cheaper and economical to outsource to countries where the cost of living is about the third the price of any first world English country.

Writing should be done locally, however. The English language is a tricky thing. There are so many nuances that native

English speakers take for granted. Whether it's a certain spelling, a phrase or a certain type of humor.

Let's take Apple as an example again. They employ some of the best copywriters in the world. Their advertising is second to none. They certainly make great products, but much of their success can be attributed to their marketing. They don't outsource that to other countries. If you want to be a marketer, it's a good profession to start with. A lot of successful marketers and businessmen start off as copywriters and grow into managers of large marketing firms.

I've expanded my business to become the head of a full digital marketing agency. I now sell everything from websites, SEO services, to apps to social media services. But I still write my own copy because partly I enjoy it, but also because I haven't found anybody who can do it as well as I can. (I know I sound like a cranky micro-managing business owner but so be it.) Becoming a good copywriter is hard. It's not about just stringing a bunch of words together. It's about triggering those psychological desires to produce an action.

If you are a great copywriter then you should be able to sell anything. If you've watched the Wolf of Wall Street then you saw the two scenes where Jason Belfort tells his friends to sell him a pen. If you put what I teach you into practice you'll be able to sell anything to those who are buyers — that means they have the need and the resources. And once you can sell, you can do anything and be anything. If there is one thing you take away from this book it's that you should become a better salesperson. Become a rainmaker. And I'm not just talking about selling a product but selling to your friends, family, your spouse, but most importantly to yourself. Yes, the most important person you need to sell is yourself. Your head is full of negative thoughts and you need the internal salesperson to get rid of those thoughts so you can be the best copywriter ever. But we'll get more into that later.

On Success

If you want to succeed in the copywriting field it's very simple. You need to read and write a lot. As one of the most successful writers ever, Stephen King, said,

"You become a writer simply by reading and writing. You learn best by reading a lot and writing a lot, and the most valuable lessons of all are the ones you teach yourself."

No truer words have ever been spoken. You can learn grammar and the different types of sentences but to truly master the craft you need to have an open mind and be willing to try new things.

Gary Halbert, one of the most successful copywriting legends of all-time also believed that to be a good copywriter you needed to read and write a lot.

If you never write, you never learn.

One thing about writing sales copy is that nobody judges you on your spelling and grammar. Sales are the only thing that matters. If you're writing sales copy and you're not very good with punctuation and spelling, don't worry too much about it. If you're trying to write the next great novel then, sure, focus on grammar and punctuation but first I want you to learn the psychology of selling and buying. That is the most important thing. You obviously don't want to send out unprofessional work but let it stop you from doing the work. Those things will come with time.

It would be great if I could offer you a shortcut to writing success but the truth is that there isn't any. There is only practice and hard work. Read everything you can get your hands on. You should study advertisements and emails but you should also study pop culture. Look at what's playing on television. Look what's online, look what's playing on the radio. Soak it all in like a sponge. I won't tell you to stoop so far low as watching the Kardashians but be aware of what's going on. You can't sell to people who you don't understand.

John Carlton calls this the "writing muscle" Carlton is one of the best freelance copywriters out there and is often called the most ripped-off writer on the web and for good reason. He is praised by the biggest names in copywriting. If you haven't checked out his training I would encourage you to do so.

On the Tools of Writing

We will cover the foundation of writing briefly here. The amazing thing about copywriting is that you don't have to have perfect English all the time. You don't need to be a grammar Nazi to be a good copywriter. You might remember as a kid having to write essays or book reports or tests, and then getting them back from your teacher all marked up in red. I don't know but you but that still gives me shivers just thinking about it. There are different types of grammar. There is good, the bad, and the ugly. We'll go over them briefly here.

Good grammar is the type that your seventh grade English teacher taught you in high school. It's using nouns, verbs, and adverbs correctly. It's using active voice instead of passive voice. It follows all the rules. You mainly use proper grammar if you're writing business reports, or technical writing. This is how we communicate when we want to appear authoritative.

Bad grammar is when you intentionally break the rules for a fact. There is an old saying once you've learned the rules you can break them. That is certainly true when it comes to writing. Using bad grammar is usually more fun than being proper. Great copywriters use bad grammar to drive a point home. Many famous writers use bad sentence structure. One of the most famous examples is from Charles Dickens:

It was the best of times, it was the worst of times, it was the age of wisdom, it was the age of foolishness, it was the epoch of belief, it was the epoch of incredulity, it was the season of Light, it was the season of Darkness, it was the spring of hope, it was the winter of despair...

from *A Tale of Two Cities*

I could just read those sentences over and over again. Couldn't you? We all remember studying that in English class. Anybody can follow rules, but it takes a true genius to use the rules and bend them for a certain effect. William Shakespeare was known to break the occasional rule. Okay, so he broke a lot of them. He created 1,700 words, changing nouns into verbs, and verbs and adjectives and inventing new words altogether. He connected words never before used together, adding prefixes and suffixes sometimes.

Ugly grammar is when you unintendedly make a mistake. Ugly grammar isn't great, but it's not the end of the world like some librarians might have you believe.

On What Books to Read?

Don't worry too much about what to read. You'll find the right books at the right time in your life. The important thing is to always keep learning and reading. Once you believe you know everything there is to know about writing or any other subject for that matter, you're be left behind and hungrier, younger writers will take your place in the food chain. It's survival of the fittest.

You don't always even need to read business books or books on writing. Don't forget to have fun and read something light every once in a while.

My favourite books on copywriting are by Dan Kennedy. He writes the No B.S. Series. His book The Ultimate Sales Letter is also a masterpiece. The other one you should read is No B.S. Direct

Marketing and as a bonus No. B.S To Time Management. I've never read anything that describes Time Management quite like he does.

Another great one I would suggest is The Advertising Solution by Craig Simpson and Brian Kurtz. It's a little more updated with updated examples which might help if you don't' think the old books are relevant anymore. (HINT: they most definitely are!)

I could go on and on. There are many great books and I would suggest you read all of them.

You're not about to win a Nobel peace prize or be knighted by the Queen of England for your copywriting. If that is your goal then do something else. Copywriting is simple and direct. You should not write complex Dickensian sentences. It is how well you communicate and how compelling you are to the reader that matters.

Copywriting is not even really about writing. Anybody can string a couple of words together. The most important part about copywriting is the research. If you're an amazing researcher but can't write worth a crap, you can still be very successful in the business. You don't even need to be that smart. Nobody has ever accused a copywriter of being a genius. (Sometimes copywriters call themselves genius but that's a matter entirely.)

On What is Copywriting?

Copywriting takes on many forms and most people have a slightly different definition. If we're talking about direct sales copywriting, then it is simply selling through words, as explained earlier.

There is also something called SEO copywriting. In SEO copywriting your goal is more to educate your reader than sell them something. It is more the art of the soft sell. SEO copywriting helps with your branding purposes, to establish an authority, and to rank high in search engines.

Copywriting is about understanding the product and the person you're trying to sell to. Whether it is your own product or service or if it is somebody else's. The good news is you don't have to have a fancy degree or be a genius to get into copywriting. Like any other piece of writing you don't have to get it right the first time. Marketing is all about testing. Anybody who says they are a genius marketer and know everything is lying. It's a constantly evolving field, full of excitement and challenges. What I'm going to teach you here is not so much marketing principles but timeless knowledge about your prospects. These principles have been used to sell to people for thousands of years and will be the same ones used in centuries to come.

On Know Thy Customer

We will be talking more about the psychology of your customer later, but we will do a brief overview here because it's so important. Your mission is simple. You must, in some way, make your customers' lives better through information, service, or a product. That is why your customers buy from you after all. They buy a knife because it cuts, they buy a car because it gets them from point A to point B, they buy a jacket because it keeps them warm and dry. Now that's not to say that there aren't secondary benefits. For example, people want to look cool driving their car or look good in their clothes, but never forgot customers don't care about your product, they only care about how it makes their lives better.

If you're making your customers' lives worse by not adding value you may get away with it for a while – even a couple years even – but in the end your business is not sustainable.

If you don't know your customer, how can you possibly sell to them? It's almost funny how often we don't know basic information about our own customer! We know the latest tricks of the trade with Facebook advertisement, Google Adwords, Wordpress but we hardly ever do a deep dive into our prospect. We see them walk into or shops or email us but that's about as much research that many of us do.

If we don't understand them, how can we persuade them to motivate them to buy something? It's about knowing where they hang out both online and off-line, what lingo and jargon they use, their annual income, and what drives them. This is more than just creating a customer persona. It's about getting into the heart and mind of your customers. It's your duty to find out much as possible about who would benefit most from your product.

Whatever you write, you want to focus on your customer. In the famous "Real Beauty" campaign by Dove, the advertisers didn't focus on the benefits of their product or why they should buy Dove soap. Instead, they focused 100% on the consumer and their body image. The campaign was created after three years of strategic research about how women view themselves. They found only 4% of women found themselves beautiful and Dove wanted to change that perception. By focusing on the customer and doing the research they were able to create one of the most powerful campaigns ever. Dove is now forever associated with empowerment and self-esteem.

This takes guts to pull off. First, a lot of money had to be spent in the front end before even the first billboard, video, and ad is ever seen by the consumer. However, this is research on your customer that you should be doing anyways. Secondly, most company brass understand the customer wants benefits, not features – it's the old saying "they want a hole not a drill" but companies aren't comfortable letting their product speak for themselves. They feel the need to add benefits just in case the customer isn't smart enough to connect that the drill is cordless and can fit a wide variety of heads etc, etc. but Dove didn't tell the consumer that their soap will moisturize the skin, clean the pores etc.

Most companies believe that they couldn't ever create a campaign focused completely on the consumer. That maybe their product couldn't' be associated with a good cause like self-esteem and image, but if you dig deep most products and services you can come up with away.

On a final note, about this, a company might object to spending that much money on advertisement but can you put a price tag on the Dove "Real Beauty" campaign. The video alone went viral and was viewed 114 million times, shared 3.74 million times across 110 countries in 25 languages. The team responsible for the campaign estimate it touched over four billion people worldwide. Let's just think about that for a moment. four billion people. Not only that, but the campaign doesn't expire. Dove can repurpose the idea for new advertisements and reach and inspire new people. Coca-cola, De Beers, Gillette, Apple and Nike know you can't put a price tag on the best campaigns.

Of course, you want to put advertisement dollars on campaigns that work. To get the most bang from your promotional buck, you need to find new customers who will stick with you and to do that you need to send out very targeted mailing whether it's through direct mail or email or through advertisement such as Google Advertisements. You don't want to send your mailing haphazardly to people in general. That be a waste of money you want to invest and efforts into the vapour best prospects who are they and how do you find them?

Your best bet for finding great prospects is to find people who are just like the people who are already proven to be consistent buyers – your existing customers. But how much do you really know about your existing customer base other than the fact they seem to like you and your products? How old are they? What is the income? Did he have large families or do they live alone? Do they own or rent their homes? What type of jobs or careers do they have? What set of hobbies and interests are important for you to know all this because if you want the best buyers than all you have to do is find other people who are just like them and chances are they will turn out to be your best buyers as well.

Take a moment to list out everything you know about your buyers and if you don't know the above questions to a survey. More pick up the phone and asked them. If you have developed a good rapport with them they will be more than happy to answer your questions. Make sure you have a broad range of answers from different customers because if your focus group is too narrow and the answers will, of course, be skewed. If you have your best customers in your Facebook Page then you can get excellent data on them without too much effort.

This book collects all sorts of useful information about your prospects take a moment to look through the and analytics and gather as much information about them as possible and then use that information to target the same type of people. Facebook has a remarketing tool that you can use to create like audiences which is super powerful to attract your ideal customer but you can also do it the old-fashioned way such as networking or referrals from your best customers.

Put together a list of features benefits

You want to brainstorm what is good about your product, what the outcome is going to be and the unique selling proposition. You want to list every possible future benefit than organize them by importance.

Sometimes there is something called the hidden benefit this is something that is not necessarily prevalent at the beginning. Sometimes it is too big of a concept to fully understand with simple sales copy. For example, you might go to a nutritionist to help you eat better. That would be a benefit. But what might actually end up happening is you would have a more productive, happier lifestyle. Of course, people want a better life but often times they don't realize how much better it can be. Another example is somebody might want to double their income. That would be a tangible result. But really they just want again a happier more successful life. It is important to think about the hidden benefits but often they are not the selling point you start off with. They are not concrete or specific enough.

Put Together a list of Pain Points

It is unfortunate that fear is often the most powerful motivator for sales. Just look at politicians. How often do we vote for somebody because we don't want the other person to get in? It's the same for a product or service. We're scared that if we don't look or act a certain way then we will miss out, that we won't be fulfilled.

As human beings, we are hardwired to avoid fear and pain as much as possible. It is an evolutionary trait that we cannot get rid of. Even when we know that overcoming fear will make us more successful in the long run. A lot of human existence is all about avoiding fear and pain which ironically makes us unhappy because we don't get the things we desire or want. As copywriters, we can use that fear to help us sell. It is the metaphorical fight or flight response. It is what spurs us into action a lot of the time. If we can detail the amount of pain a person will be in if they do not buy our product then that is 85% of the battle right there.

Just as he did with the features and benefits list the pain points the potential customer will be in if he or she does not buy your product. You can then rearrange them based on importance. The pain points can often be more difficult to convey than features but if you can do so succinctly and accurately you will become an amazing marketer. Remember that people would rather avoid pain than feel happiness. It sounds strange but true. Why does the guy not ask his crush out? He's afraid of rejection even though the upside maybe years of bliss, maybe even marriage and a life partner. Think of all the missed opportunities you've missed out just because you wanted to be comfortable.

For Beginners

If you're just starting out then this section is for you. If you're experienced and would like to get into the gritty details then you can skip this part and get into the mindset of a copywriter. But I think there are some lessons for copywriters who've been at it for a while so read on.

The name of the game is traction. You need to get the first couple of clients but once you get those you can leverage them into other clients by using testimonials and referrals. But getting those first clients is always the most difficult, sometimes it can take months.

As you start your freelance career, you can't afford to turn down any work which is why I suggest you try to learn as much as possible and broaden your skillset.

Copywriting is a hard skill to sell to clients. A lot of people think copywriting is just doing a bunch of writing and anybody can do it. That it doesn't take any special skill to write copy for a website or an email which is probably why so many are so awful. When you're starting out and don't necessarily have the marketing skills or the knowledge to find the people you need to.

The best thing to do is pair up with a web developer or a graphic artist who needs help with the writing. Often these businesses rely on the client to do the writing and the clients are way too busy to do the work so the projects get delayed. These can be ongoing strategic partnerships.

It's important when you're starting out to decide what your market will be and what your specialty is.

As a rule of thumb, you're better off becoming a specialist than a generalist, that is until you make a name for yourself and build up your client list. There are all kinds of specialties you can choose from but if you have some experience it is beneficial. For example, if you edited a pamphlet for a software company then maybe you should start with tech and make that your specialty.

The highest-paid niche is probably writing promotions, direct mail and online for consumer newsletters. That is basically multilevel marketing, travel, health, and investment newsletters. Those guys pay more than just about anyone. However, don't choose something just because it could pay the most. You need to be knowledgeable and passionate about the subject. Another good niche is writing for healthcare, particularly alternative medicine, nutritional supplements. Pharmaceutical and medical advertising is also very lucrative.

Speech writing is another non-direct marketing area you can consider. It's difficult to get into because there isn't a lot of work out there for speech writers, unless you live in Washington D.C. or Ottawa or London but is fun and pays well.

Pick a niche within your specialty, which means what type of service or product that you are covering, what industry, and also what are you writing for them. If you pick computers, are you only writing data sheets or are you writing websites? What are you going to write for these clients? If you tell me I want to specialize in writing copy for people that read about Russian History, then you have a problem because there won't be enough jobs out there for you.

The second thing is find and identify good lists of prospects in those areas. Maybe there's a trade association that has a local chapter where you live that you should go to and network at and become a member of. Maybe there's a newsletter or a magazine subscription list you should be renting. Identify how you're going to reach these people.

If you determine that your market is marketing directors of pharmaceutical companies then you need to figure out how to reach them. There are many ways to do this but probably the most effective is through LinkedIn where you can learn their company name, position and you can contact them directly. With LinkedIn, it's easy to scrape a list together of qualified prospects. Copywriters of the past would have given an arm and a leg for the information we have at our fingertips.

The third thing I would do is I would contact them and guess what, direct mail is still extremely effective despite what all those internet gurus will have you think. There are other methods that people advocate today.

If I were starting out today, that would still be the first thing I'd do. I've composed a really good lead generating sales letter to generate inquiries from my copywriting services and then mail 500 to a list of prospects in my market and then wait four or five weeks and see. I do other things during those four or five weeks, but see what happens.

If that letter works and you can get a 1%, 2, 3,4 5% response, you're going to be able to fill the pipeline with leads and if they're good leads that percentage of them is going to reliably convert to business and you'll be set. If you can generate a steady flow of sales leads and you can create a sales letter that every time you mail 100, you get 3 good leads or 5 or 2, you're really not going to ever have to worry about having business as long as there are sufficient lists and your market is broad enough.

On Networking Events

I can't stress how important networking events are, especially when you're first starting out. It can be a bit of a long game but sometimes you fall into some business right away. Don't get discouraged if it takes some time for you to get known. If you don't have any clients I would try to go to as many as five or six networking events to begin with. (Yes, that many). I've built most of my business on networking events. I met my business partner at a networking event.

Business Networking International (BNI)

I was lucky enough to join a Business Networking International group, the biggest in Canada which helped propel my career. I've gone to hundreds of different networking events and this is by far the best. If you've never been to a BNI you'll know that this is where all the serious business people hang out. BNI you're encouraged to bring in at least four referrals a month and all your stats are tracked, including how much business you generated for your chapter. Visit a couple of chapters and see where you best fit in. For someone starting out especially, I would highly recommend it.

On Board of Trade or Commerce

You should find your local Board of Trade or Commerce and join it. It's good to get as much visibility as possible in your local business community. If you can, volunteer for events to give yourself that much of a boost. Go to their tradeshows, go to their events and just get your name out there.

Other Networking events are good. I would try and find early morning meetings rather than evenings. Why? It might just be my personal bias but evenings have a couple of things against them. First, they tend to be more social. If they are serving booze I would run the opposite direction. The second thing I found about evening networking events is that they tend to attract the not-so-serious entrepreneurs. The people who still have a day job and don't want to leave the comfort of their steady paycheque. Nothing is wrong with that but they are unlikely to be the client you want.

On Social Media

As mentioned previously, LinkedIn is your best friend when it comes to social media. It's the best place to make B2B connections. Because copywriting is such a specialized skill and one most people don't realize they need, it's often best to align yourself with a web designer or a marketing agency. In the beginning of my career, this was my bread and butter. They could often refer you repeat business. However, whatever you do, don't spam people on social media.

You're there to be social and you have to let relationships happen organically.

On Google Advertising

I'm a big fan of Google Advertising (formally Google Adwords) and have gotten a lot of my clients through them. If you live in a small town without much business then this could be a great way to get a few clients. It's definitely harder if you live in a town of a thousand opposed to one million. The great thing about Google Adwords is that you can control your budget so try putting $5 a day and see what return you get. If you find it works for you then increase your budget accordingly.

On The Art of the Referral

One of the least used tactics is to ask your current clients for a referral. If your client is happy then ask them who else they know that could use your service. Often they know somebody but they obviously aren't concentrated on your needs. It sometimes just takes a little brainstorming and an email introduction to get a new client!

On Cold Calling

This is most people's least favourite way of getting new business (including mine). And is probably your last resort. I wouldn't recommend cold calling businesses without doing some research on them first to see if they are looking for a copywriter. The type of businesses you want to target would be small marketing firms who don't have a full-time copywriter or a web developer.

Copywriting is a much-needed skill that isn't going anywhere. Need to work hard at your craft be dedicated. Study great copy, great advertisement, and great websites. Look at the best mail campaigns and see what they're doing right.

On Clients

The chapter on selling covers how to get clients in detail so I won't talk too much about it here. If you decide to go the freelance route to pick up clients then you'll need to spend a significant part of your day networking, and looking for new clients.

Gary Halbert, one of the greatest copywriters of all time, had a saying "client suck." He once had a seminar down in Key West Florida. He filled the room with potential clients and other copywriters. The admission was over a thousand dollars a ticket. He showed up to this seminar 15 minutes late wearing Hawaiian shorts, football jersey and a hat that said 'clients suck.'

He proceeded for the next 20 minutes deluxe in the room follow hit ideal clients with the ways that his copywriting client suck. How they think they can edit and how they screwed up his. How they can't strategize and knew nothing about selling. He said he made far less money from his ads because clients wouldn't listen to him. How if he had been running the ads himself he would've done a much better job. He told the crowd how much he hated clients how much he'd rather not ever work for another client again how no one could pay him enough money to do more client work. Do you think people got up and left? In fact, it was the opposite. People kept handing him cheques for the entire weekend.

Now this is a rockstar mentality that I deftly would not recommend this approach until you become a 'rockstar'—and even then I wouldn't recommend you be a complete idiot about it. But it does show up on time and be respectful of everybody around you. If your client does indeed suck, you have my permission to tell them and not to put up with their bullshit (excuse my French). You have to remember each time you do something extra or go that extra mile to make them happy, it's a lost opportunity cost. It may be worth it for your good clients but it may not be.

On Your Target Market

Whether you are just starting out or have been a copywriter for some time, it's always beneficial to establish or re-establish your target market because it can change and should change over time as you become more experienced.

If you're a new copywriter, you should go for the low hanging fruit basically web designers who need help producing copy for their clients. Once you become more established you can target the more sophisticated companies that are running promotions for complicated products.

Your target market is the group of people you serve. For example, could be tech startups who have one to five employees and are at Ground Zero with their marketing plan. Once you've established that you can market towards that niche.

If I had a penny for every time I heard people were afraid that they were to rule out some of the clients because their target market was too narrow I would be a rich man. It is always better to start small and expand then to start large and then have to contract. By having too broad of a target market, you will be lost in the sea of your competition. No matter how much she liked to be everything to everyone is just not possible even if you could be you could be doing a disservice to yourself and your clients in the attempt you can serve your clients a better by being more specific narrowly focused.

If you are packed with clients then now may be a great time to look at your target market again. Are you completely happy with the level and quality of your clients? The chances are you can be getting clients that offer you more money for less at work. Perhaps you want to go after that dream client that he hadn't thought possible that maybe was just outside of your reach.

On Branding

For any business, branding is probably the most important distinction you can make. It's what helps you stand out from your competition. It makes you unique. My favourite copywriting company brand is Men with Pens. If you go to their website you can see that they are distinct from any other copywriter. They are not just one in 1000 different copywriters. They are hip, funny and don't take themselves too seriously. They stand out because of their branding. As you can see branding doesn't necessarily mean that they're better just means that you're different from your competition. What makes you different from your competition? People who can't establish a brand work on Upwork for $10 an hour. They have to cut on price because they can't show the value of their services another way.

Think about your personality and what makes you unique. The good thing about branding is you get to be yourself especially as a solo partner don't be afraid to put yourself out there. One of the greatest copywriters of our time Ben Settle has a unique voice and although he might not consider himself an expert on branding, he certainly has an amazing brand.

I would recommend you subscribe to his email list and find out how he writes to his audience. His emails and very male centric. He talks about picking chicks up and about how crazy women can get. These emails can be very offensive to some of his audience members. But the great thing about his brand is it's not supposed to speak to everybody. A brand speaks to only a segment of the population.

When people create brands they are scared that they will exclude part of their target market. But I have news for you: Not everybody is going to hire you. Not everybody wants to hire you. Just because you target a specific niche doesn't mean you have to

One of the most admired marketing agencies is called Taxi. Their website is www.agency.taxi. Brilliant. I love it. Now, why would you name a digital marketing agency, taxi? It certainly stands out from the competition.

Let's look at Apple again. It is obviously a very distinct brand that is marketed towards hipsters, artsy people and creative's. But now everybody buys Apple because they want to be seen as young and hip. Apple products are more expensive because they know it's almost a fashion statement to own an apple product.

Even if you work in a big company you need to have a personal brand. It doesn't matter if you're an entrepreneur or not. The person who hires you going to do so or not based upon your personal brand.

On Unique Selling Proposition

The unique selling proposition is a part of branding and is what makes you a fit for your target market. It's something special that you offer that sets you apart from other copywriters and from your competition. What guarantee can you offer your clients? Your USP should be clearly stated on your website and when you sign up a new client it should also be a part of your onboarding process. This is something that you guarantee will get done and something that your competition does not offer.

An example could be a hundred percent satisfaction with the result and unlimited rewrites until the client is happy. But maybe you don't want to offer that it is too rewrites for start charging extra. A contractor friend of mine has a guarantee that he won't go 10% above his quoted price, otherwise he will pay from it from his own pocket. A business coach I worked with offers the guarantee that if you don't increase your income within six months you will work for you for free until he does. These are excellent guarantee because it assures the customer that they are getting value for their dollar. If you have a great USP then it allows you to charge premium dollars for your service.

Chapter Two:

On The Mindset of a Copywriter

A copywriter should have an understanding of people, an insight into them, a sympathy toward them.

– George Gribbin

This is the most important chapter in this book, and perhaps the most important chapter ever written about copywriting. I only say that because to be good at anything you need to first think you're the best. You need to have the mental fortitude before you can have anything else. It's also a short chapter because there isn't much to it. All you need to do is go out there and take massive action.

This chapter will help you become a top-rated copywriter and if you want to go on and become the best in the business then you need to read and reread this chapter. There are two parts you need to manage, the internal world and external. You can't manage the external world without first mastering the internal first which is why we're starting with mindset.

One thing you should keep in mind while going through this chapter is everything that has been accomplished by humankind is possible, you can accomplish it. The reason you haven't yet is because of a limiting belief you have. At first, I know this sounds ridiculous. How is it possible for you to become a neuroscientist or an astronaut? You might say, as I did for so many years, that you're bad at math. That your brain just doesn't work that way. I'm here to tell you that you just haven't developed that side of the brain. You are capable as anybody else on this planet. Just remember that.

To be successful you really need to look within yourself and figure out what is blocking your way. What is preventing you from going out and becoming the best writer possible? In this chapter, we're going to look at several things that are preventing you from being successful. Remember that the things that prevent you from being successful aren't the things that you know because if you knew them already you would just fix it and go out and do it.

The thing that is prevented you from being successful are the things you don't know what you don't know. Take a moment to reread those words again because I want you to guide your entire life by that simple principle. You don't know what you don't know. In other words, you have no idea why you're not succeeding and if that's driving you crazy figuring out then this section is definitely for you. Sounds simple right? If it was everybody would be happy, rich and successful.

On Body Sensations vs Higher Ideal

We all have instances in a life where are told or are shown in some way or another that we are not enough. How insecurities as humans then take hold and prevent us from breaking through the clutter.

It took me a long time to realize how much fear was ruling my life. And oftentimes it was manifested in subtle ways like trying to always look good in front of people. Because I was always trying to look good I never was able to truly express myself and what I wanted.

I urge you to look at where fear is holding you back not only in your business but in your life. Because I guarantee that where you stopped at one place is also the very thing that is stopping you in other areas of your life. For example, if you want to get married and you are not even going out on dates it will most likely stop you from getting new clients as well.

One of the hardest things to do is to get over the fear of rejection. It's unfortunate you have to go through 10 or even more rejections to get one yes. There is that old saying that a no just means you're one step closer to a yes. I know it may sound cliché but this actually does help. With the global village, it's much easier to reach out and connect with people. If you truly believe that your copywriting skills will help businesses then you have to go out and try to sell as many people as possible. We will talk more about selling later but really most of selling comes from mindset and once you have a basic grasp of these concepts selling will become a lot easier. The mechanics of selling are not difficult it's just that most people are not very secure about their cells and their own abilities.

How do you get over the fear of rejection? Ejection really is just fear expressed in a different way. It is the fear of not being good enough. Strange that we always seek approval of others. To strange human traits that we seek the approval of others to make ourselves feel better about ourselves. But really no amount of affirmation from the outside will make one bit of difference in your mind. Your self-image and self-worth I would help you to either succeed or not. If you think you're not good enough and you go out and try and accomplish something your mind will be racing in the background the same old track of I'm not good enough. It will be little actions you take or don't that will stop you from achieving your full potential.

It takes a lot of courage to go out and lead the life that you want. I believe most writers probably suffer from more than their fair insecurities and fears. Not sure if insecure people are drawn to writing or if writers are just naturally insecure.

If you feel crippled by fear you're in luck because overcoming that fear is like a muscle. I remember publishing my first novel and I was crippled with insecurity. I didn't want anybody to read it. I was too scared to even sell it. Our brains are great at self-sabotaging ourselves without even realizing it.

What do you get out of self-sabotage? The reinforced belief that you're enough and you're worthy of all the riches and happiness.

On Your Experiences

When we are younger, something your parents told you was that the world works in a certain way and we took it to mean something – usually negative. Maybe it was that should not play with your brother or sister's toys and we made it believe that our parents didn't love us as much as our brother or sister now we forget about this feeling consciously but subconsciously we carry that feeling around with us all we go and we interpret everything as we are not lovable.

This greatly affects our ability to succeed in life. If we always believe were not lovable and we will self-sabotaging ourselves. We will think that we not good enough or not capable. Once we realize how limiting we are we have the ability to free ourselves and express ourselves fully. Will you know you and you know he can what to

If you lack self-confidence in a certain area, say your ability to write, a good exercise is to make a list of all the things you can do to become a better writer. It might be practising writing more or reading more or even taking a creative writing class. When you realize you have all these options and you are able to take them then your self-confidence will grow. It's only when we think that something has to be a certain way and we only have one or two options do we become fearful and how self-confidence shrinks.

To be a master, you must have all these things in place. If you are timid and lacking in confidence it will show not only in your writing but in getting new clients are talking to your boss. You will not be a merciful copywriter until you master yourself.

On Fear

We talked briefly about fear but we're going to go into more detail here.

Remember our brains are not designed to make you happy. They are designed to help you survive. They protect you from the world.

We are all ruled by our flight or fight mechanism our early ancestors developed in order to stay alive. It is so engrained in our body that we don't even recognize it when it comes up. For example, let's say you're in danger of losing a client. You feel scared because it could mean a loss of income for you or it could mean that you failed or maybe you make it mean you're not a good enough writer or marketer or whatever.

We have two choices when faced with fear. The first one is to run away and avoid the feeling and the entire situation. We've all experienced this when we get the credit card statement in the mail. We don't want to look at it and shove it under junk mail. The other is the fight mechanism is not is when we get angry and start yelling and screaming and throwing fits in order to get what we want.

Unfortunately, neither of these reactions are in reality and don't do anything to help us deal with the situation at hand. Only by realizing where we use the fight or flight mechanism to deal with situations can we begin to see how it is limiting us in our actions. If we avoid the credit card statements then we don't actually take any actions to pay it off. Neither does creating a scene help us to you with the situation.

How does this help in copywriting? Often we will avoid going after what we want because we are afraid of the reaction we will get. We want to feel rejected or not good enough so we like to deal in this fake world instead of looking at things from a reality-based perspective.

What happens if we really are not good enough for Mark then at least we can deal with that and take steps to improve our writing or I'll sales techniques are something else. But by constantly avoiding that feeling you will never improve. Just because we're not where we want to be doesn't mean we're bad or useless. We like to come up with alternative feelings and emotions around not being where we want to go remember well not good enough at some point rather and allies that something but don't let that stop you and don't let the feelings overwhelming. Continue to take the actions you know you need to do regardless of how you feel about. Do not let the fight or flight mechanism get in your way.

Jordan Belford tells this amazing story in his seminars about the time he was getting his helicopter's licence. To pass the test, he had to turn off the engine and freefall then turn the engine back on and pull up to safety. This was to ensure if anything did go wrong then he would be able to think under pressure. Belford's instructor said the key to successfully achieving this manoeuvre was to look up into the air as you are pulling up on the throttle and not look down at the ground.

You need to look into the future and not be paralyzed by fear at what is happening at the moment. Jordan thought this would be pretty simple: just look up into the sky. But when the time came to pull up he found himself looking down at the ground that was rapidly coming closer and closer. He was so afraid of the ground that he wasn't able to pull off the maneuver.

His instructor had to start yelling at him to pull up a look into the sky. Though he knew what to do, his body tightened up and was unable to do anything. His instructor made him do it a second time. This time he knew he wouldn't have any problems.

He knew exactly the feeling and body sensations that were preventing him from succeeding. He turned off the engine again and he started stalling, falling to the ground and again his mind was so conditioned to be looking at the threat in front of him he couldn't pull up. It took him three times to be able to pull off the manoeuvre. The problem is that as human beings we can only look at the threats that are in front of us. The problems that are immediate that we cannot come up with solutions. We tend to be stuck in the present unable to imagine a future that is any different than the one that is hurling towards us. We only see impending doom and can't look around and see the options we have to change our lives.

May not be the master writer you want to be right now but if you can look in towards the future and imagine success as you want it then you will achieve it. I'm sure you've heard about how athletes visualize success. They will

On Being an 'A' player?

Most people believe they're not an 'A' player because of their limiting beliefs. They're happy to be in the middle or bottom of the company's sales. They are not making enough money because deep down they don't believe in themselves or don't believe they are worth more. What distinguishes an 'A' player from a 'B' player? Simply knowing that believing that they are best in their field and what they do. Are you the best copywriter and you act like that whenever you're in front of clients or with coworkers?

This may seem a bit hokey but if you don't believe you're in an A player then get up five minutes early in the morning dress sharply like you're ready to conquer the world and stand in front of the mirror and repeat to yourself "I am the best copywriter in the world". Most of the battle is mental. The skills and knowledge can all be learned easily enough.

Everything you need to know about copywriting is in books. A lot of information you can find for free on the internet. I wanted to learn how to code and I was astonished to learn that everything I needed to learn I could find for free online. You don't need to spend $10,000 on a coding Bootcamp anymore. Money is no longer a barrier to a higher paying job. You can acquire all the skills you want and need. So why do people still complain about not having enough money? It's because they don't truly believe they are worth more money. It's easy to complain they don't have enough money, but what they're really complaining about is that they don't feel confident in themselves to go out and get more money. They believe that their self-worth equaled their paycheck. If they had more self-worth they would realize that they weren't being paid enough and would go out and do something about it. It's all about mentally conditioning yourself to think and act like the best.

Another trait of top copywriters that they take their destiny in their own hands they don't allow external forces to stop them or find excuses that prevent him from succeeding. If you're reading this you have the tools to change your life and be the person you want to make take the money you want. All you have to do is go get it.

On Writer's Block

I have to wonder who came up with the idea of writers' block. When did it become a thing? Why is it widely accepted among writers? Is it just an excuse to not do work? I think in a lot of cases it is to perpetuate the romantic idea of the long-suffering writer.

But I've also known writers who have suddenly unable to write. So what causes writers' block and what is it? There are many different explanations but I think it comes from when a writer's mind is just too overloaded with the stimulus that they can put the words down on the paper. I know this may seem a little contradictory since you might think that if you had too many thoughts, you would be able to capture at least some of them on paper.

When you're writing you need to have a clear mind to be out to concentrate on the work at hand. But if you're having health problems or your writing with your spouse that it's really hard to concentrate on writing.

Writing is a skill, don't kid yourself on that. People who are born talented writers don't understand what it's like with other people when it comes to writing. It takes a level of concentration that is the only very difficult for most people. Most types of work you can to when tired, you can push through student, but you can't with writing. It's best the musts you hop yourself up on caffeine, to this get a good snipes rest.

When we can't fully concentrate then we call the writer's block is solution is to empty your mind of everything except for what you need to read about of course this is easier said than done most times. If you having a hard time the best practice is meditation. It will help you clear all thoughts from your head and be able to concentrate on what's important.

The most important part of any writing job is just a start. It can seem daunting to sit down in front of the computer and start writing. But once you do that the words will start flowing easily.

Chapter Three:

All the Psychology You Need to Know to Become a Master Seller

The best copywriters are the most tenacious researchers. Like miners, they dig, drill, dynamite, and chip until they have carloads of valuable ore. John Caples advised me once to gather seven times more interesting information than I could possibly use.

- Gary Bencivenga

Countless products and services are being offered for sale 24 hours a day. There are many messages bombarding people every day. This includes Facebook, mail, magazines, Instagram TV ads, Youtube, and billboards, just to name a few. Whenever you're selling in whatever medium you choose there is one consistent that's critical to the success of any advertisement or promotion. You have to know what your customer is thinking and feeling. Next, understand the psychology of your ideal customer and then look at your product or service from their point of view. These are just some of the questions you have to ask yourself before you even write a word. Before you even think about writing.

- What motivates them?

- What keeps them up at night?

- What are their greatest fears?

- What are their greatest desires?

The greatest copywriters in the world understand how to make a prospect take action. The ability to use their knowledge of human psychology to create amazing marketing campaigns is what makes them so highly sought after and bringing in the big bucks. Many marketers don't have formal training in psychology; they just pick it up along the way

A great copywriter knows how to interrupt somebody's patterns and thoughts. This concept is straightforward and simple. It's about getting your reader whoever he or she is to think about your product or service.

On Emotion Vs Logic

This is extremely important to understand for any copywriter and marketer and salesperson in general. Before you start writing your first draft, you want to think about what sort of emotion you want to convey. What you want the reader to feel? What is their emotional state before reading your ad and what do you want to change? Although logic is important, it is an emotion that will make the sale.

Of course, you have to be logical, because however are you going to convince your spouse that was a good purchase? A lot of the time, people will even sell themselves using logic. (I really want it because it will help me do XYZ better) But it really comes down to the emotional component of the product (I really want it because it makes me feel successful.) How does something make you feel when you have it?

Why do people buy the latest iPhone even though they have a perfectly good working one at home? Why do people buy a BMW when a Honda will get them there in the same amount of time? It's certainly not a logical decision; it's an emotional reaction to how the product makes you feel. Apple might be the best company and arousing emotion in their customers. You can tell just by how many diehard fans there are for Apple products. They wouldn't be caught dead using Windows. Few other brands inspire that sort of loyalty, especially these days.

The reason I love M&Ms and pizza – which I usually have as a treat once a week – is because I remember as a family sitting around the TV every Saturday night watching a movie having pizza and eating M&Ms. It was our ritual. The thing we did together. This simple purchase brings me back to my childhood, when my entire family was together.

You must feel to bring readers to point when they feel they must do whatever it is you seek to get them to do. Whether that's to buy, sign up for email list or some of the action.

Take Coke's 1971 commercial "I'd like to buy the world a coke" that also played at the very end of Mad Men, for example. It is considered one of the best television commercials of all time and not because some announcer told you a list of facts about how Coca-cola is the best soft drink in the world. It's because of the way Coca-cola makes you feel.

The advertisers behind Coke marketing are brilliant because if you look at all the logical reasons to drink it, there are very few. Sure it might give you a caffeine and sugar buzz, but it also rots your teeth, is over 5oo calories per bottle, and if you believe some reports, is a good engine cleaning agent.

If Coke used logic to sell its products it would be bankrupt. Their products aren't all that good and they are terrible for your health. But the company that popularized the modern image of Santa Clause is a master at playing on people's emotions. In "I'd Like to buy the world a Coke" there are people from all over the world singing together. There are hippies, business people, Africans, Indians, and many others preaching unity and harmony. People naturally want to be part of that movement.

We're not as logical as we'd like to think we are. Most of our decisions are based on deep-rooted emotional motivations, which we then justify with logical processes. So, first help the right brain create desire, then satisfy the left brain with features and hard data so that the wallet actually emerges

When you research, think about the emotional reason why somebody would buy that product. If, for example, you're in the health and beauty industry than what about your products makes your customer feel and look different than before? Does it give them confidence? Does it raise their self-esteem? What about it will improve their lives and help them achieve their dreams or desires?

Whether writing sales copy for email a webpage or direct mail sales piece before you ever put one were down on people you should decide what effect you want to have on the reader. You must know the feeling you need to row so that prospects will be moved to take action. Course you have to be subtle and not over the top or cheesy about it. People don't want to feel as though the emotions are being manipulated.

As I said before, they want to believe that their decisions based on logic. The challenge of the right is to present arguments that seem to convince intact while in fact all of its aiming at the motions. That's how you compel people to take action. It takes a lot to get people over the initiate of just sitting there doing nothing being comfortable as opposed to getting up and doing whatever is required to attain whatever it is you're selling and they want. It takes a lot to get something to consider spending money on anything. Even motivating people to click through to your website takes special effort.

You need to convince people that they will feel much better as a result of doing whatever you ask them to do. For example, most people know that eating healthy food is good for them but you can't make people buy vegan meals just by putting them on the counter. You need to make them feel like they are healthier, and they are saving the animals, and the plant.

I remember back when I worked at Starbucks people would always ask why we didn't have anything healthy to eat but whenever we brought in a healthy food item it would sit in the food case going untouched. People thought they wanted healthy food but when it came to actually making the purchase, they always chose the emotional product – the unhealthy cookie or muffin.

As a marketer, a good place to start is with yourself. Ask yourself what we'd get me over the inertia so I would take action and buy. Even if you are not your target market that is a good starting point because you know your own emotions and logic the best. It's not always to stare into the soul of your prospects and know their every feeling and desire, but I would say you probably know yourself pretty well.

Of course, starting with yourself is good but it shouldn't end there. You have to find out what your prospects want above all. Do some investigating talked to the people who already know and who are the best buyers for your product.

The power of the internet allows marketers to do infinite research, gather huge mounds of data and use this information very quickly in meaningful ways. However, nothing beats picking up the phone and talking to somebody. Form focus groups. That way you can hear the intonations of their voice and understand them as people a little better.

On Triune Brain Theory

The Triune Brain theory has been out of fashion for many years now but its theories still hold some useful lessons in advertising and sales. People have been trying to understand brain function and development since as long as there have been humans. But it was Eugene Schwartz who pioneered the idea in marketing and sales in the modern era.

The Triune Brain Theory was first proposed by doctor and neuroscientist Paul D. MacLean who formulated the model in the 60s. According to MacLean the brain has three parts, the reptilian, the paleomammalian, and the neomammalian complex. It was wildly introduced to a broad audience by Pulitzer Prize winner Carl Sagan. Recently the reptilian rain theory has been championed by Seth Godin.

The Triune Brain Theory has several important lessons which is why we're covering it here. We all think we are rational people, doing things based on logic and we can provide a rational nation for everything we do. However, that rational decision is just a cover-up for our more basic emotional instincts. We do not like to think that we are governed by emotions. Rather we make these decisions and then cover it up with logic telling ourselves that it was the right thing to do so we can feel good about ourselves.

Eugene Schwartz socked through this flattering self image saw the deeper motivations that underlie many out decisions and buying actions. Schwartz said there are three levels to our brain function and they go from high to low.

On The Reptilian Brain

The reptilian brain, as it's called, is the oldest part of the brain. It's the intelligence center that has enabled life to survive in its varied forms for millions of years.

The reptilian brain's job is to keep you safe and alive. That's it. It's not meant to make you happy or satisfied or deal with complex human emotions. First and foremost among the traits generated through the reptilian brain is the fight or flight mechanism that drives us all. All those things we do each day that we don't think about are driven by the reptilian brain. When you look both ways to cross the street it is your reptilian brain kicking in. Sexual urges all come from the reptilian brain. When you scratch an itch or instinctively know how to get home from work without thinking about it. Even how you chew and swallow your food is your reptilian brain taking over.

The reptilian brain fundamentally influences our behavior and controls body functions required for sustaining life, such as breathing and body temperature. Repeating patterns such as rituals, automatic responses without conscious thought, predictability, fear of losing job, or spouse, or home, or dying, lack of money & resources, and the unknown are all response created by the reptilian brain.

Once people are in fear of not surviving the reptilian brain takes over and we are at the mercy of its reactions to perceived threats.

It is thought to represent a fundamental core of the nervous system and derives from a form of mammal-like reptile that once ranged widely over the world but disappeared during the Triassic period having provided the evolutionary link between dinosaurs and mammals. All modern mammals have this reptilian complex, including humans.

On The Paleommalian Brain

The second brain evolved over the reptilian-like brain is the paleommalian brain. The paleomammalian formation, or limbic system as it is often called, should not be confused with the midbrain. Forebrain, midbrain, and hindbrain are terms designed to help describe developing embryonic brains. In triune brain theory, the midbrain is actually part of the protoreptilian formation.

The prefix *paleo-* means *early* or *old*. Mammals, as most of us know, came into existence after reptiles were already crawling the earth but *before* primates began swinging from tree to tree in forests.

The palemammalian brain adds behavioral and psychological resolution to all of the emotions and specifically mediates the social emotions such as separation distress or social bonding, playfulness, and maternal nurturance.

On The Neomammalian Brain

At last, we come to the neomammalian complex (or cerebral neocortex). This third part of the brain is represented in the hand model by the fingers and top surface of the hand. This part of the brain is unique to primates. There is also an even more highly evolved brain that is unique to humans. The neocortex is responsible for things that make us distinctly human: logic; reasoning skills; higher-order thinking skills such as analysis and problem-solving; speech and verbal understanding; meaning-making; willpower; and, wisdom..

Cognitive therapy (also called cognitive behavioral therapy) often encourages people to leave the past in the past, and instead focus on the present or the here-and-now. While these sorts of interventions are helpful for some things, they are not particularly helpful for trauma integration. Cognitive therapies or any reason-based interventions primarily target the prefrontal regions of the brain (logic, reason, and time awareness). However, it was the limbic region of the brain that was activated during the original trauma to help the person survive (through flight, fight, or freeze). During traumatic experiences, when the limbic brain is activated, the prefrontal lobes go offline. This makes perfect sense from a survival perspective. You can't reason your way out of tiger attack. For a person in crisis or intense emotional distress, whether in real time or in response to triggers from earlier, unprocessed experiences, no amount of reasoning will help.

So why would any of us attempt to appeal to a part of the brain that isn't really "on?" For optimal healing to occur, all three brains must be able to work together. Neurologically, unprocessed trauma creates disconnection in the brain. If this sounds alarming complex, don't panic. You will not need a team of experts to devise ways for the three brains to work together. Pause here and take a nice deep breath. Great! All three brains worked together during that slow deep breath. Deep breathing might be considered a whole brain intervention. Breath originates in that primitive reptilian region of the brain. Likewise, any movement-based or body-based intervention automatically works within the limbic and reptilian brains.

Each of these brain levels are important to make decisions and how people live their daily life. Back in caveman days, they were used for our survival. According to Schwartz, we function primarily from the higher brain level for the lower levels brain not always running in the background, sort of like a computer system. Schwartz described the lower level brain function as the reptilian brain or chimpanzee brain. Schwarz said we are only a slightly more advanced version of the chimpanzee. If you look through the evolution of time and Earth's history our evolution is fairly recent in the grand scheme of things

On a subconscious level, our reptilian brain is always trying to keep us alive. It is helping us breathe, it holds your hand away when you touch a hot stove, it is on the lookout for traffic when you cross the street. It's always taking in these signals that we don't necessarily register.

So although a lot of how conscious mind is filtering out advertisements but you'll be happy to know that unconsciously we take in this information even though we don't necessarily process it. According to Schwartz, it's not the higher functioning brain that makes decisions but the lower levels. The reptilian brain is reacting and then deciding.

This can be challenging because, as a writer, we need to appeal to both levels of the brain. Let's say someone reads a website about a secret on how to look 20 years younger. The reptilian part of the brain loves this idea. Who wouldn't want to look 20 years younger, especially if this person is perhaps recently divorced and now is looking for a new romantic partner? But the high level functioning side of the brain knows he can't possibly be a secret to make itself look 20 years younger, otherwise everybody would be using it and it would be a secret for very long.

If you are the copywriter then you have to come up with something that sounds reasonable to the high-level still appeal to the reptilian brain. You need to strike the right balance between the two. Only when both parts of the brain are harmonized will you get a sale.

So instead of the secrets to making yourself look 20 years younger, you can come up with a headline that looks like this

Finally! Learn How a New specialized, anti-aging cream, will make your look and feel your best in under two months!

Now may not be the most compelling headline but at least it appeals to the lower and higher parts of your brain. For starters the headline doesn't promise too much. Today's consumers are so cynical because they have seen so many ads they're not going to believe anything that over promises even if they can deliver.

On Motivation

We also must understand the motivations behind people's buying habits. If you can't find what persuades them then you'll never be old to sell a product or get them to do what you want. Put yourself in your customers' place and try to determine the prospects prime motivation for buying. Again you'll need to do research on your potential customer and find out what they want and why they wanted.

In preparing your sales materials you'll need to turn that motivation into a spark to make your prospect take action immediately, if possible.

The term pattern and trapped rigidly stems from something called Nero linguistics programming.

A pattern interrupt is a very powerful sales technique that any professional, regardless of industry, can use whenever they are speaking to a new prospect.

As humans, we are trained throughout our life to deal with almost everything how we are taught to deal with it or have learned to do the past. Almost every action we do in life is from some programming we've had. We are not sure the program to tune out any commercials or advertisement we see. Even if we want to see an ad our mind tells us to shut down and think about something else.

For example, if somebody is sad our natural pattern is to comfort them. We still have the old fight or flight mechanism that largely governs our behaviour. When we encounter an obstacle we still basically have those two options. Let's say you're boss has just denied you a promotion. You can stomp around and get angry and start yelling which is the fight mechanism. Or you can accept it and go back to your normal job which is the flight mechanism.

Let's say you're making a sales call. The person on the other end has years of experience dealing with salespeople. The normal pattern would be to answer the phone, the salesperson would ask them how they're doing, introduce themselves, make a pitch. Because nothing unexpected happened both parties acted in the usual way and the salesperson was most likely unsuccessful. As soon as the person on the phone recognizes he is talking to the salesperson he lapses into his normal way of being.

As a copywriter, it's your job to interrupt somebody going through their every day life. Most people have pretty mundane lives so if you can somehow jar them out of it then you're most likely be successful. People wake up, have coffee and breakfast, complain to their spouse and then go to work. These people are begging for your help. They are begging for you to make their lives better and it's your job to go out and do it. If that doesn't help motivate you to go out and get more clients, write better sales copy then I don't know what would.

Tony Robbins is very successful at jarring people out of their normal thought patterns. He will often swear and say something outlandish in order to get his point across. Now, I'm not telling you to swear in your emails or sales letters but if you can say something different without being offensive or distasteful than you have a leg up on your competition. People see the same sales message over and over again. Fifty percent off this, closing out sale there.

On State Change

This is a technique that was originally popularized by Neuro Linguistics Programming or NLP and the basis of it is that you control how you feel and react. Most of the time we are governed by an external stimulus that we react to and therefore will change our state. For example, if a beloved pet dies in my family then we will naturally feel sad. This is an external event that we react to and changes our emotional state. However, we can actually separate the external stimulus with our emotional state. Through this practice, we can actually learn how to control how we feel. It takes lots of practice to not be governed by external forces and sometimes it may seem impossible, but you have a choice of how you respond in any given situation.

How can you master your state and how does it apply to copywriting? Let's say you want to feel confident going into a client meeting. But you are afraid and nervous that you will not say the right thing or you will screw up in one way or another. How can you change that? Think back to a time when you felt the most confident.

You want to slow the memory down so you know exactly what you're seeing, what you're touching, what you're hearing, and even maybe what you're smelling. If you can associate a certain motion with a smile it will make it that much more powerful smell is actually an underutilized sense. What was going on around you?

I felt the most confident when I won a Table Topics competition in Toastmasters. Table Topics is when you give a two-minute impromptu speech from a surprise question. I remember the Table Topic master looking at me holding out the ribbon with both hands and calling out my name. I ran up to the front gave her a big hug. I remember the huge smile on her face. I felt like a real winner and very powerful.

You really want to feel your body sensations and what was going on with you at the time and replicate that at will. By replaying this in my mind I'm able to conjure up confidence whenever I need it for a client meeting or a sales presentation.

I know this may seem a bit strange but if you do it enough then the feeling will become automatic. After a while, you will be able to just use the body sensations to bring back that competence and not have to go back and imagine the event all over again but it takes practice. This will help you in gaining more clients and being out to sound more confident in any meeting that you have with them. Being able to shift your mind will not only help you in your professional life but your personal as well when you realize that you do not need to be influenced by outside sources or events that happen beyond your control.

On How To Change Habits To Sell Anything

Can you imagine getting up or going to bed and not brushing your teeth? It used to be the in the early 1900s almost nobody had formed the daily ritual of brushing. In fact, during World War One the US army stated that poor dental hygiene was a national security risk when they found so many recruits had rotting teeth.

How did the United States go from chronic tooth decay to it being unthinkable to skip a day brushing your teeth? It was the famous advertising man Claude Hopkins, who wrote the classical book On Scientific Advertising, and who persuade the nation that it was important to brush the teeth.

Claude Hopkins was already a well-known advertising executive when he was approached by an old friend who had a business idea for a toothpaste he created called Pepsodent. He believed that the marketing opportunity was huge and requested Hopkins help him design a national promotional campaign.

Claude Hopkins had built a huge reputation by turning dozens of unknown products such as Quarter Oats, Goodyear Tires, and Van

Camp's pork and beans into household names. Hopkins friend believed he could do the same with Pepsodent.

Hopkins who would be known as the father of evidence-based, data-driven approach also wasn't one to ever let the truth stop him – bending and exaggerating when it suited him. He convinced people to buy Schlitz beer by boasting that the company cleaned their bottles with steam, while neglecting to mention that every other beer company used the exact same method. He had dubiously claimed that Cleopatra had used Palmolive soap but that didn't stop it from flying off the shelves.

Although there was an opportunity for dental hygiene as there was unprecedented teeth decay as the heavy consumption of sugary processed foods was rising to Hopkins also knew that selling toothpaste would be a difficult sale as almost nobody was using it. It's one thing to get somebody to use a new product but to get somebody to start a new habit is incredibly difficult.

Getting someone into the habit of brushing their teeth isn't as easy as it might seem today. Why wouldn't someone brush their teeth? But we don't do a lot of things that would be good for us like eating a piece of fruit a day or taking vitamins. Creating a new routine is incredibly difficult and nobody knew this more than Hopkins.

If they were to be successful, he would have to cultivate an entire new routine Hopkins agreed to create a campaign for his friend if he gave him a six-month's option on a block of stock. It would be the best financial decision he ever made.

Within five years of the partnership, Hopkins turned Pepsodent into one of the best-known products and in the process helped create tooth brushing as a daily habit.

Hopkins who was the pioneer of taking a structured, calculated approach to advertising first defined the problem and then offered a solution. The science behind Pepsodent was he found a certain cue and reward that fueled a particular habit. It's a connection so powerful that many advertisers still use the cue and reward system to promote their products.

Hopkins crated a craving that made cues and rewards work. It is that craving that works to create a habit loop. The Habit Loop is a neurological loop that governs a consistent behavior. It consists of three elements: a cue, a routine, and a reward. Understanding these elements can help in understanding how to effectively advertise and write copy for We often think of cravings as bad – as when we indulge in sugar or alcohol or caffeine – but we also have other cravings.

To sell Pepsodent, Hopkins needed a trigger that would create a need for the toothpaste's daily use. Like any good advertiser, he did a lot of research on the subject and found a reference in the middle of one dental book to the plaque on teeth which he called "the film". This "film" would eventually be the cue. You could run your tongue across your teeth and feel the film. This gave Hopkins the idea to advertise toothpaste as a beauty product, not a health product. (Remember what I said early about selling using emotion, not logic?)

He advertised Pedosdent as a product to deal with the cloudy, yellow film despite the lack of medical evidence. He decided that the "film" or plaque as a cue could trigger the habit of teeth brushing. Soon the nation was plastered with Pedsodent ads.

Note how many pretty teeth are seen everywhere. Millions are using a new method of teeth cleaning. Why would any woman have dingy film on her teeth? Pepsodent removes the film.

Hopkins had found a cue that was simple and had existed for ages and was an easy trigger that an advertisement could cause tooth brushing to become a habit. The reward was, of course, to be more attractive – one of the oldest rewards in human psychology. After all, who doesn't want a beautiful smile?

The campaign was later reinforced with television advertising. The very popular Pepsodent jingle is still very much in the collective conscious, even today.

You wonder where the yellow went, then you brush your teeth with Pepsodent!

Within weeks of the start of the campaign, the demand for Pepsodent exploded. The company could not keep up with the orders that were pouring in. Within a decade, Pepsodent was one of the top-selling brands in the world and remained America's best-selling toothpaste for more than thirty years. A decade after Hopkin's ad campaign went nationwide, over 65 percent of Americans used Pepsodent. What is more by the end of World War II, the US military downgraded concerns about recruits' teeth because so many soldiers were brushing their teeth every day.

Hopkins took advantage of the habit loop but ti wasn't until almost a century later that science would fully understand why habits exist and how they function. Hopkins created a toothbrushing habit by identifying a simple and obvious cue, delivering a clear reward and by creating a neurological craving. The reward that Hopkins identified was hard to resist. He had used the same reward he had with the Palmolive Soap: to look beautiful.

All habits, no matter how large or small have three components. There's a cue, something that triggers the craving and the routine.

Unlike other toothpaste of that period, Pepsodent contained citric acid, as well as does of mint oil and other chemicals. Pepsodent's inventors had used the ingredients to make his toothpaste minty and sure the paste wouldn't become gluey as it sat on the shelves.

These chemicals gave the teeth a tingling sensation on the tongue and gums. When researches at competing companies interviewed customers, they found that people who had used Pepsodent missed the cool, tingling sensation in their mouths if they didn't use the toothpaste. This slight tingling sensation was the craving. If it wasn't there, their mouths didn't feel clean.

Claude Hopkins wasn't selling a toothpaste. He was selling the craving to be beautiful. Once peopled craved hat cool tingling which they equated with cleanliness and beauty, brushing became a daily habit.

Did you notice one conspicuous thing in the 1929 Pepsodent ad featured above? Hopkins gave reasons in the ad why readers should try Pepsodent, but he did not attempt to sell them. Instead, he offered a 10-day trial. By doing offering a trial period, he removed all the risk from the consumer.

Chapter Four :

The Art of Selling

Why waste a sentence saying nothing?

- Seth Godin

I've always hated the saying, "selling snow to Eskimos. It implies that selling is about getting anybody to buy anything. The truth is great selling isn't about forcing something down somebody's throat. Getting an Eskimo to buy snow is nearly impossible, and way too much work. You need to first find out what people want and then sell them that. Do you have an Eskimo as a customer? Sell them a heater instead. It's a lot easier and more lucrative.

Selling is the most important skill you can ever have in your entire life. You're doing selling all the time even when you don't realize it. In fact, every transaction you have can be perceived as selling. This can include even talking to your friends. Let's say you're with the group and you want to go to a particular restaurant. In fact, this happened to me just the other day when I had a gift certificate to an Italian restaurant and I had to convince my friends to go there even though there was no benefit for them. That is selling. In fact, this is so important that I have dedicated an entire chapter to selling. But you need to read the second chapter on mindset before you can sell anything.

I'm sure you've gone into a shop and had somebody try to sell you some sort of top-of-the-line product without even knowing what you want. To be a successful salesperson you need to first, as Stephen Covey famously said, "seek to understand."

Without first understanding the needs of our customers you can't help to sell them anything. You first need to ask them a lot of questions and guide them into making the correct decision that is best for them. You can't jump in with sales spiel about why you're the best copywriter for the job.

Start with a line of inquiry about what the client is looking for and then present your skills in a way that best meets the client's needs. You need to dig deep, go beyond the surface of what the pain the selling is facing. Show you can find a solution for them. Take the client down a pathway without doing any direct selling, allowing the client to come to their own conclusion that you're the best option for them.

It's important to research your potential client before starting your line of inquiry which is extremely simple to do in today's world. All of your clients will have an online presence. Google their name and company and find out as much about them as you possibly can before you start talking to them. It's a salesperson's sin to ask your potential client a question that you could have found out about them online.

Selling is really like peeling back layers of onions and asking good insightful questions. Your potential client won't be truthful with you right away. They'll give you almost any objection of why they can't hire you because with any purchasing decision there is a lot of fear associated with it. The first objection they give you for not hiring you — most likely they can't afford to — probably isn't the real one. Keep peeling back the onion and don't get dejected because inevitably, they will say no.

On You Work For Yourself. Period

The biggest mistake you can make as a copywriter — or any profession for that matter — is to think you work for anyone but yourself. Even if you're technically an employee, from the time you enter the workforce to the time you retire, you're self-employed. You are the president of your own personal corporation, selling your services into the marketplace at the highest price possible.

According to one study, researchers found that the top 3 percent of people in their field looked upon themselves as self-employed. They treated the company as if it belonged to them personally. They saw themselves as being in charge of every aspect of their lives. The people who take control of their lives and don't blame others, even in the slightest are the ones who are the most successful.

They don't blame others for bad days, for failures, for clients leaving them for somebody else. They realize their destiny is in their hands. That the sale is entirely in their control, whether they like it or not. That nobody else can make them succeed or fail.

It's human nature that we blame others for our problems in our lives. We naturally don't like to take accountability because it means we've failed in some form or another and we don't like to admit it. But as soon as you accept that somebody didn't hire you or buy from you then the faster you'll be able to learn and grow. If you can just master this one skill then you'll be happier and wealthier.

This sounds simple on paper but it's incredibly hard to do. Your spouse cheats on you and immediately you think he or she is a horrible person who deserves to die a long, terrible death. But what did you do to cause that behavior?

Your first response, no doubt, is "Nothing. I was a perfectly upstanding citizen." But, here is the part you don't want to hear, I guarantee you did something. I'm sure it was inadvertent but you did something to cause your loved one to cheat on you. If you shift your entire perspective and look at what you can control then it will change your entire life. So next time you suspect your spouse of cheating, don't spy on them or hire a private detective, look at your own behaviour and see what you can change to make you the best possible spouse so nobody would ever dream of cheating on you. You can't control your spouse's actions, you can only influence others through your own.

It's a fact I, unfortunately, forget all the time. Just the other day a client cancelled on me. I immediately called her and left her a voice message. She didn't return my call so I called her again and then texted her. Still no reply. I thought to myself "Not a lot I can do if she won't communicate with me."

But that is incredibly disempowering. I was blaming her for firing me when it was my responsibility to provide the level of service she expected. It was my job to get through to her.

You'll have clients cancel on you all the time. Instead of being angry and bitter about it, look at it as an opportunity to grow and see where you're lacking.

Dammit It, Jim, I'm a Writer, not a Sales Person

I hate to break this to you but you're a salesperson in every aspect of your life. Whether it's convincing your significant other or your spouse you are the person of their dreams or that your kids should brush their teeth, everything you do has some kind of sales component to it. Copywriting is all about convincing somebody to take an action. Copywriters usually know all the sales techniques, but aren't charismatic enough to pull them off in real time in front of an audience. Alternatively, a salesperson is a great talker, is passionate, and charismatic. They can stand up in front of a hundred, a thousand, ten thousand people and sell them.

- Language
- Mindset
- Tonality (confidence)
- Dress
- Closing techniques

To be able to sell yourself as a high-class copywriter you need to master two things: empathy and ego drive. Empathy is the ability to feel as somebody else does and to see things in their shoes. Having empathy does not necessarily mean being sympathetic. One can know what others feel without agreeing with that feeling. But a salesperson simply cannot sell well without the ability to get powerful feedback from the client through empathy.

A salesperson with good empathy reacts to the customer and is able to adjust his or her tactics based on those reactions. He or she is not bound by a prepared sales track but functions in terms of the real interaction between them and the customer. Sensing with the customer's feeling he or she can change pace, tone, double back on his or her track make something clear, and modify when necessary to hone in on the target and close the sale.

The second quality you need to be a good salesperson is the kind of ego drive that makes them want and need to make the sale. Getting a sale boosts confidence not merely for the money but for the thrill of it. It must give a boost of adrenaline. In effect, top salespeople and top copywriters have to provide a powerful means of enhancing your prospect's ego.

The salesperson must think he or she is the best at what they do, and believe that a client will generally improve their life with their product or service.

The person with a strong ego maximizes motivation to fulfil utilize whatever empathy he possesses. Needing the sale, he or she is not likely to let his empathy spillover and become sympathetic. The ego needs to make the sale. On the other hand, the person with little or no ego has a hard time to use empathy and a persuasive manner. He understands people and many know perfectly well what things you may say to close to sell effectively this understanding is apt to become a little too sympathetic.

There is a dynamic relationship between empathy and ego drive. It takes a combination of the two, each working to reinforce the other—each enabling the other to be fully utilized—to make the successful salesman.

It calls for a very special, balanced ego to need the sale intensely and yet allow the salesman to look closely at the customer and fully benefit from an empathic perception of the customer's reactions and needs.

Thus, there are a number of possible permutations of empathy and drive.

On Handling Objections

The ability to handle objections is key to how well you are successful as a salesperson. Almost every prospect you come into contact is going to shut down at the beginning. Do not feel rejected by this because buying a very scary experience. The larger and more expensive product is more scared there prospect is going to be and the more reasons your prospect will find to not do anything. It is almost always more comfortable to stay put than to move forward and experience something different. Remember your last serious relationship? I bet you stayed in it longer than was good for you because you were scared of change. You were scared of trying to find someone new.

The most common objection you will hear is your service is too expensive or they cannot afford it. This is the most common objection because it is the easiest one to say and covers up a whole array of other objections that your prospect just doesn't want to admit. The truth is that your prospect and almost always forward your services if they need them bad.

The next time someone tells you that your service is too expensive remember that it's a lame excuse. It's lame because it means one of two things; that they don't see value in what you do or you don't provide enough value. You have to figure out which one it is. If it's the former, then all you have to do is to figure out a way to communicate your value, and if it's the latter, you just need to figure out a way to provide more value.

On Failure of Tests

By know, I know what you're thinking. Can't I just hire a salesperson while I do the writing? You can have salespeople, you can have ten, twenty, a hundred salespeople, but if you aren't your own best salesperson then you'll never succeed in getting clients or hiring great salespeople to help you.

A top salesperson is enormously valuable, and if you're building an organization, it is the single most important task. More important than branding, more important than strategy and more important than having a great product.

So how do you find that invaluable person? It's not something they teach in schools. You don't hand out grades for being a world-class salesperson.

For at least 50 years, psychologists have been working hard trying to figure out what traits are the best ones to have. Almost every aspect of human personality, behavior, attitude, and ability has at one time or another come under the scrutiny of the tester. There have been some notable successes in testing, most especially perhaps in the IQ, EQ. and mechanical-ability areas. Of late, personality testing, especially with the increasing use of projective techniques, has gained a certain level of sophistication. The area which has been to date most barren of real scientific success has been aptitude testing, where the aptitude consists of personality dynamics rather than simple mechanical abilities.

John Carlton is a master of what I call the "muscle writing." He can write a brilliant ad on any subject, no matter how complex. Yet, he makes each ad easy to understand. Also, he writes it in such a way, it's as impossible to stop reading as an Ian Fleming or a John D. MacDonald novel.

'It's all about the idea'

Every piece of work needs an idea but, in most cases, the idea isn't even half of it. Imagine Ricky Gervais is pitching The Office to the BBC. The idea, he explains, is a dull bloke who works in a dull office surrounded by dull people and not much happens. How do you think that meeting would have gone? Exactly.

What made The Office or Seinfeld or Frasier so brilliant was – of course– the writing. Creative departments are seldom run by copywriters. "Creatives" are now in charge of creative departments. They may call themselves executive creative directors or chief creative officers, but very few can call themselves writers. I'm not saying this is better or worse. But what happens when a piece of copy is presented to one of these ECDs?

If it's brilliant or terrible, don't worry about it. He and she can recognize that and will either approve or reject it. However, most copy is neither brilliant nor terrible. It's somewhere in the middle. There's usually room for improvement. But if the ECD lacks the writing skills to improve it, how will it ever get better?

On Everyone's a Writer Now

Every desk has a keyboard. Everybody types, so everybody writes. Account handlers, clients, construction workers… everyone. In an unfortunate perfect storm, this has coincided with the decline of writing skills in creative departments. So creatives have surrendered their once-proud ownership of the written word. Yes, everyone's a writer now. Except, ironically, the people who are supposed to be.

You used to be able to start in an ad agency as a junior copywriter but sadly it's not respected as a skill anymore. People go into coding bootcamps instead. Coding is the new copywriting. This is just the way the world is right now – which is okay, (coding is just writing in another language, after all) but nobody respects writing in plain English anymore.

Business owners don't understand words still have power, a lot of power. They think they can razzle dazzle their clients with fancy designs, animation and those things do create a wow factor. But remember it's your words – both written and spoken – that will get your client to fork over money.

On Headlines

There are four important qualities that a good headline may possess. They are:

1. Self-Interest
2. News
3. Curiosity
4. A quick and easy way …

Advertising can never become completely accurate or 100% scientific because of the human element involved. In advertising, you are dealing with emotions of human beings, and these will always be, to a certain extent, unstable and unmeasurable.

That is why it is necessary to test, test, test — to test copy, media, position in publications, seasonal variation, and time of day in broadcast advertising.

On Sales Strategy

A lot of freelance copywriters and business people, in general, is they don't have a sales strategy that allows you to repeat your work and get predictable results as well as scale up if you want.

Creating a sales strategy is easy it's sticking to it is hard. It's having the mental fortitude to be able to handle rejection and disappointment which is why the mindset chapter is so important. If you believe you're the best you won't feel put off by rejection you won't think that there's something wrong with you rather do something wrong here potentially lead.

On You Customers For Life

Once you have a good customer, you should hold onto them for dear life do not let him go. You should never give up on them even if the don't have the budget. Some customers have fired me because I'm too expensive but they almost always come back to me.

I have an acupuncturist client who I was writing a script for and midway through production, he said things weren't working out. I told him no problem and we left on good terms. About six months later, I learned that the marketing team that took over stole $2,000 from him and delivered nothing. The acupuncturist called me up and he is now a client again.

Getting new customers is incredibly costly and time-consuming. As a salesperson you might have a tendency to go after the new clients and not pay attention to present ones thinking that they are happy and content. Instead of looking for new clients consider looking for ways you can upsell your present clients on new services. How can you add value to what you're ready do?

Read your clients from 1 to 10 on how much they are engaged in your work. Do they return your calls? Do they ask questions? Do they follow up with you? Yes, when you don't hear from a client for a long time and they seem disengaged, that is when they leave you.

To prevent this from happening when something happens give him a call even if it's something minor. Come up with an excuse to keep in contact with them. You should be in constant contact with every single day and make sure that they are well cared for even if it's for only a brief conversation.

If you take good care of them and they are happy and then there's no reason that customers should ever leave you.

Chapter Five :

The Big Idea and Research

*I never desire to converse with a man who has written more
than he has read."*
– Samuel Johnson

You won't always get the big idea for every marketing campaign
and you don't necessarily have to have one to be successful, but if you
plan to be a world-class copywriter then you'll need to try and reach
for the stars. Every marketing campaign you remember had a big idea
attached to it.

We had a big idea of buying a Mclaren with bitcoin for our
client Active Pay Solutions. This was just at the beginning of the
bitcoin craze when nothing like this had ever been done before. It was
sure to cause waves. Active Pay is a marketplace for bitcoin payments
which cut out credit cards and other vendors which typically take
around a 3 percent fee

We just had to find a dealership that was game. We found Drive
Motorsports, a high-end dealership that dealt in luxury cars. I still
remember our clients came to pick us up in a Porshe Cayenne as we
drove to the dealership.

It was the first time I had ever seen a bitcoin payment made and
I was fascinated by the process. We took pictures all around and got
the transaction done (I couldn't believe it had only cost 45 bitcoins)
and were the recipient of one Mclaren. Pity I didn't get to keep it.

The entire campaign was a complete success. We got published in some major newspapers and got some great PR buzz for the company.

When you think or marriage or an engagement, one of the first things you think about is the ring. It is an emotional symbol of love and commitment.

In fact, it's worth at least 50% less than you paid for it the moment you left the jewelry store. And yet, we feel compelled to buy them for our loved ones anyway. The man is expected to get down on one knee. How did that become the norm? It's hard to imagine that it's only been three-quarters of a century since diamonds became the symbol of wealth, power, and romance they are in today's society. And it was all because of a brilliant, multifaceted marketing strategy designed and executed by ad agency N.W. Ayer in the early 1900s for their client, De Beers.

In what is the most brilliant marketing campaign of all time, over the course of a few decades, N.W. Ayer helped De Beers successfully turn a failing market into a psychological necessity, all during a period of war and economic turmoil.

How exactly did N.W. Ayer convince Americans that diamonds are the ultimate symbols of love, romance, and marriage? What were the marketing campaigns that turned the diamond industry around?

De Beers' 80-year stronghold on the diamond industry was one of the most impressive and fascinating in history. Let's take a critical look at how the company used marketing to create and manipulate demand for diamonds from nothing.

On How It All Started

Diamonds haven't been rare stones since 1870, when huge diamond mines were discovered in South Africa. Soon after the discovery, the British financiers behind the South African mining efforts realized the diamond market would be saturated if they didn't do something about it. They succeeded to monopolize diamond prices by creating De Beers Consolidated Mines, and taking full ownership and control of the world diamond trade. While they stockpiled diamonds and sold them strategically to control the price, De Beers Chairman Sir Ernest Oppenheimer cultivated a network of wholesalers all over the world.

When De Beers began looking for an ad agency, the global economy was suffering and Europe was under threat of war. Their challenge was to figure out which country or countries had the most potential to support a growing diamond market, and then to hire an agency to implement a marketing campaign in those countries. Because of Europe's preoccupation with the oncoming war, the U.S. was chosen -- even though the total number of diamonds in the U.S. had declined by nearly 50% since the end of World War I.

N.W. Ayer did exhaustive market research to figure out exactly what Americans thought about diamonds in the late 1930s. What they found was that diamonds were considered a luxury reserved only for the wealthy and that Americans were spending their money on other things like cars and appliances. To sell more and bigger diamonds, Ayer would have to market to consumers at varying income levels.

So, how do they get more people to buy big diamonds in a bad economy? They needed to figure out a way to link diamonds with something emotional. And because diamonds weren't worth much inherently, they also had to keep people from ever reselling them. What was emotional, socially valuable, and eternal? Love and marriage

N.W. Ayer's decided to create a situation where almost every person pledging marriage feels compelled to acquire a diamond engagement ring. It was an ambitious goal, for sure. How were they going to achieve it?

The concept of an engagement ring had existed since medieval times, but it had never been widely adopted. And before World War II, only 10% of engagement rings contained diamonds. With a carefully executed marketing strategy, N.W. Ayer could strengthen the tradition of engagement rings and transform public opinion about diamonds -- from precious stones to essential parts of courtship and marriage. Eventually, Ayer would convince young men that diamonds are the ultimate gift of love, and young women that they're an essential part of romantic relationships.

On Creating the Story

You should always have a story you tell your clients. And you should use your clients' stories to sell to their clients. People connect with stories. They remember stories and they tell their friends stories. When you start with any marketing campaign you should always think about what kind of story you want to tell.

We had the story of buying a luxury car with a new type of currency. De Beers wanted to make it look like diamonds were everywhere, and they started by using celebrities in the media. N.W. Ayer's publicists wrote newspaper columns and magazine stories about celebrity proposals with diamond rings and the type, size, and worth of their diamonds. Fashion designers talked about the new diamond trend on radio shows.

N.W. Ayer used traditional marketing tools like newspapers and radio in the first half of the twentieth century. In addition to overt advertisements, they created entertaining and educational content -- ideas, stories, fashion, and trends that supported their brand and product, but weren't explicitly about it. The brilliant part of this strategy was they weren't out to sell De Beers. There was no brand name to be impressed on the public mind. There was simply an idea -- the eternal emotional value surrounding the diamond." Their story was about the people who gave diamonds or were given diamonds, and how happy and loved those diamonds made them feel.

Every one of De Beers' advertisements featured an educational tip called, "How to Buy a Diamond." The instructions said: "Ask about color, clarity and cutting -- for these determine a diamond's quality, contribute to its beauty and value. Choose a fine stone, and you'll always be proud of it, no matter what its size."

The agency saw tremendous success from its early campaigns. In just four years between 1938 and 1941, they reported a 55% increase in U.S. diamond sales. Riding this success, N.W. Ayer began perfecting their marketing strategy in the 1940s. They wanted to convince Americans that marriages without diamonds were incomplete.

"A Diamond Is Forever"

These four iconic words have appeared in every single De Beers advertisement since 1948, and AdAge named it the number one slogan of the century in 1999. It's hard to refute its popularity and effectiveness. You talk to your friends, your family, random people on the street and they have heard of it.

It's unclear why the slogan was chosen, but it was a choice that would contribute greatly to De Beers' tremendous advertising success. Even now, the URL www.adiamondisforever.com redirects to De Beers' main website.

The slogan perfectly captured the sentiment De Beers was going for – that a diamond, like your relationship, is eternal – while also discouraging people from ever reselling their diamonds, as mass re-selling would disrupt the market and reveal the alarmingly low intrinsic value of the stones themselves.

At the very beginning of De Beers campaign in the late 1930s, the suggested spend on an engagement ring was one month's salary. In the 1980s, De Beers ran a campaign to reset the norm to two months' salary. The advertising message was: "Isn't two months' salary a small price to pay for something that lasts forever?"

I know men must hate this but you have to admit, it's a brilliant strategy. The ad is telling men to spend more money on a diamond – and the kicker is that it's worked on millions of men worldwide.

From the start, De Beers and their agency created and manipulated demand for diamonds by monopolizing the market, changing Americans' attitudes, and convincing people that a marriage isn't complete without a diamond ring, turning it into a social norm.

De Beers knew their product wasn't intrinsically valuable like gold and silver is. So instead of marketing to their product, they mastered the art of marketing to values -- in this case, the values and ethics surrounding love, romance, and marriage.

No one was interested in buying diamonds when they conducted their first round of extensive market research, so they had to create that value themselves.

Most companies are the former, meaning they are reactive to existing value – like when Kraft Foods, Inc. changed its marketing strategy when market research showed a consumer attitude shift away from direct promotions of junk food to children.

De Beers was part of the latter camp -- their agency's market research showed a major decrease in demand for diamonds, so they executed marketing campaigns that would shift, rather than accommodate, those existing social attitudes. While brilliant and successful, it also opens up a ton of ethical concerns.

It's fascinating how De Beers and N.W. Ayer created demand from nothing by coming up with a story and value proposition around their product – and it's still successful today.

Since the turn of the century, De Beers has effectively lost its monopoly of the world diamond trade, although they still bring in billions of dollars every year. But by marketing an idea rather than a product, they built a strong foundation for the $72 billion-per-year diamond industry and dominated it for a good 80 years.

Does Every Campaign Need A Big Idea?

You don't need a Big Idea for every ad you write. Big Ideas are incredibly rare and only come around once in a blue moon so don't feel too bad if they aren't popping out of your head every second sentence.

However, it certain helps you sell your product, like De Beers. And it will vault you to the top echelons of copywriting. Because lets' face it, it's not your ability to write that will propel you to the top. Anybody can figure out how to write a sales letter or an email marketing campaign. It's the ability to be creative and to think.

What is a 'Big "dea? The Big Idea was coined by legendary copywriter David Ogilvy. It is the eureka moment which can be used to sell even the most boring products. It's the words that stop your prospect dead in their tracks.

It is a unique and compelling idea that captures people's attention and makes them want to find out more about the product or service. How can you buy a $200,000 car with just 45 bitcoin? The story makes you want to find out more about bitcoin and the bitcoin marketplace.

You should spend most of your time coming up with your big idea. In fact, don't write a word until you have that big idea. It's the most challenging part of the job. When you have the 'Big Idea' you'll know it. You'll get so excited about it you won't be able to wait to put it on paper.

There is certainly no formula for you to come up with your Big Idea. It takes hard work and dedication. But we can deconstruct the Big Idea a little.

1. **Creative** – It's something that nobody has ever thought about before. For it to be creative, you need to put two separate ideas together and make it one.

2. **Seductive** – It needs to pull your customer in. It needs yo leave your customer wanting more. It will get them to take action, whether sign up for your newsletter or buy your product.

3. **Beneficial** – The Big Idea should be something your target customer wants.

One of the most famous examples of the Big Idea is David Ogilvy's Rolls Royce campaign. Apparently, he got it from one of the trade journals and became the headline to one of the most successful campaigns Ogilvy ever wrote:

At 60 miles an hour the loudest noise in this new Rolls Royce comes from the electric clock.

It still stands as a powerful headline today. Let's deconstruct it a bit. Is it creative? Yup. It brings two separate ideas: the sound of the engine and the clock. Very original! Is it seductive? You bet. People want to know more about the Rolls Royce. What makes it so quiet? What other features does the Rolls Royce have? And lastly is this beneficial, do people actually want a quiet engine? Yes, of course, they do. They want to enjoy their drive.

Let's look at another one, this is written by Gary Halbert.

Now, at last, you can have it too!

**The Amazing Facelift In A Jar
Used By Hollywood Stars Who
Don't Want Plastic Surgery!**

Is this creative? I would say this is a little less creative than it was back when Halbert first wrote it. (Now people are always talking about Hollywood Stars getting facelifts but still, I've never heard of a facelift in a jar before so we give him half points for this one.) Is it seductive? Yes!

This is something that Hollywood Stars use. And lastly, is it beneficial. The health and beauty industry is worth billions of dollars. Everybody wants a quick and easy way to look younger.

So how do you come up with the Big Idea?

David Ogilvy said he came up with as few as 20 Big Ideas in his lifetime, yet it is considered one of the most famous copywriters and advertisers of all time. So if it takes you awhile to come up with a Big Idea for a headline and campaign. Don't beat yourself up if you don't swing it out of the park all the time.

What's the single toughest secret you'll ever learn if you hope to blow the doors off the world of writing sales copy?

For all the clever metaphors you'll ever come up with, for all the phrases and images, the formatting breakthroughs, the clever taglines, and everything else… nothing will pack more career-building punch for a copywriter… than mastering the art of coming up with "big ideas."

By no coincidence, that alone could take you a lifetime of writing. What does a big idea look like? Like anything creative, there is really no single definition of a Big Idea. You just know when you have it but here are a couple of ways to look at it: Big Ideas are the Aha Moment

Big Ideas are the Aha Moment

It's not necessarily something you can put your finger on. You know that feeling deep down in your gut? It's a feeling that just something will work out. Have you ever asked a long-time married couple how they knew that the other was the right person for them? Did you get an answer that they just knew it? It's not logic, it's a gut feeling that it's right. And just like that married couple, you'll know when you have the 'Big Idea.' There will be no doubt about it. It will just feel right.

Big Ideas are Concise Big Ideas are the Aha Moment

Big Ideas are simple to understand. The Big Idea should be no more than two sentences max, simple to digest and understand. There are so many great lines from the film Casablanca which are quoted time and time again. My personal favourite is "We'll always have Paris." It's not particularly a poetic or complex line. But it somehow fits with the wiry, bittersweet tone of the film. It sums up the film's entire theme of lost, unresolved love. That's what makes it a big idea.

Big Ideas are Timeless

Advertisement trends come and go but the essence of the big idea will remain the same. A Big Idea should stand up to the test of time. A 1,000 songs in your pocket is a big idea. Although the iPod has been discontinued the idea still holds true today as it did when the iPod first came out. Why is that? Because we still want 1,000 times in our pocket, the way that is delivered is superfluous.

Big ideas never really die. They build momentum and even if the product is no longer available the idea lives on. Even if De Beers closed up shop tomorrow, diamonds would still sell.

Another Big Idea is the Las Vegas 2002 campaign "What happened here stays here." This idea of Las Vegas being placed to let loose and do things you'd normally wouldn't do continues to this day even long after that campaign has ended. In fact, we are still talking about it even almost 20 years late.r

Big Ideas are Original

This may seem obvious, but Big Ideas are something that nobody else has thought of before. They can be a new angle or a new discovery. Remember what I said about combining two or more ideas together to make something else? That is where Big Ideas come from.

It's combining what you learned from the beauty industry with something you read in a newspaper about an airplane crash. It's putting together Roman history with a fact you learned about deep sea diving. We naturally want to read about something nobody else has thought about before. The only way to come up with an original big idea is to read a lot and be naturally inquisitive. Study, study, study and learn all you can about everything. Be a sponge of everything. Don't censor or limit yourself. Read magazines you have no interest in – if you hate football pick up a Sports Illustrated; if you have no interest in gardening pick up a House & Garden.

Big Ideas Stir Emotion

A Big Idea has to evoke emotion in your reader. Your writing should always make the reader feel something, otherwise it's flat and lifeless and uninteresting. The Big Idea should make a connection at the very core of your soul. Sometimes it actually shifts the belief system of the individual. The Big Idea must be so strong it must compel the reader to act.

One of the most famous marketing campaigns of all time, Volkswagen's "**Think Small**" advertisements is a great example of a Big Idea. It was created in 1960 by advertisement group Doyle Dane & Bernbach, and it managed to change people's entire perception about a product. Small is often considered a negative. Nobody wants anything small, and especially back in 1960 when gigantic cars were king of the road.

Another hurdle they had to overcome was even in 1960 the American population was still avoiding buying anything German. Though this one campaign, it managed to change the Volkswagen's perception

The research will tell you if you are promoting a good or bad product before you launch. If you are starting with a bad product than you're already behind the Eight Ball. I suggest you move on to a better product you can sell and they won't be a ton of returns. It's possible to sell a bad product just as much as a good product but you'll reputation will suffer in the long term. It's just not worth it to sell a bad product.

Through polling and interviews, you can learn exactly what these people think of your company. If you discover that a bad reputation is interfering with your company's growth, you now know exactly where the problems lie, and what you need to do to polish your image.

If I had a dollar for every time I was in a meeting where we were fighting over the best ad or the best copy and I would be extremely rich man. If you watch the show madmen and you may know what I'm talking about here.

Opinions and guesswork are important but they don't mean anything until you actually test it in the market. You won't know for sure until you're out in the real world. This, of course, doesn't mean that you can write up anything and stick it into the ad to test. Use your knowledge and skill. but just know that it will be only a prototype until you have seen the results.

The research will determine your target audience do you know who will want to buy your product? A lot of businesses can hone their target market and find out who is buying from them. If the company hasn't done any recent research into the target market then you should do so immediately. You may be surprised about what you find.

For example, you may think that your product will appeal to millennial's new plan to advertise to your demographic when in fact your product may appeal more to baby boomers.

A common mistake is to write copy for two target markets. A company may be targeting both the millennials and baby boomers and instead of paying you twice wants to save a buck or two and only create one landing page for example. This is always a mistake and a very common one. You should try and talk to your client out of doing this. I've worked with companies who've even used to opt-in forms for different target markets. This inevitably confuses the reader and they will click away. Focus, focus focus.

Research will enable you to jump over your competition another type of research you should be doing is on your competition. See what they're doing and see how well it's working for them he might not be of the fine all the information you're looking for let's see what you can find about them. You might be surprised at the sort of things you can find out about them

By finding out how the target market is talking about your product or service will greatly help you figure out what sort of language you should be using in your copy. If the industry that you're writing about uses a lot of jargon or big words, do the target market understand them? You may think you know what your ad is saying but your prospect may not.

Research will force you to look at the numbers hopefully you have set up some sort of analytical tracking system to your landing page for your email marketing. Most copywriters do not number people in there for the research forces them to be accountable. By looking at sales trends also you can predict to some degree how successful your campaign will be

With most campaigns, it's important to give away a free bonus, discount, or service. The research will determine what best fits your target market. For example, it might be a free phone consultation or a sampler pack. Some free gifts will be more appealing than others depending on who you are targeting.

Know becomes a success in any field without putting in the time and effort and discipline. This is especially true when it comes to writing advertising. Today with the global economy there is more opportunity than ever before but there's also more competition. You need to be better than ever before.

The internet is filled with endless information and plenty of distractions. Everybody is on the Internet which gives you a world audience but it's now even tougher to gain people's attention as people are used to short bursts of information.

To be a successful advertising anything you need to take time and dive deep into your product to learn what makes it unique or what makes it rise above the noise the trick is to find the story in the product and that takes skill. Maybe you're selling something ordinary like.

You may think that it's hard to find a story that makes bolts interesting but that's why they pay you the big bucks. Find out more you can about the company and the people that read it. Guaranteed there are at least 20 amazing stories just waiting to be heard and told.

Researching your product has always been important, but it's even now more important than ever before. With more competition and more skeptical customers, you need to ensure your message is specifically targeted to your ideal customer and accurate. You cannot exaggerate or tell a lie, even though a lot of great copywriters did so in the past (and continue to do so). The truth is only one Google away. Remember that.

What makes it all worthwhile is if you do the research you'll find the product itself in the facts. The devil really is in the details. These details will provide you with the creative ideas you need to make a successful campaign. You don't need to be a creative genius to come up with me an amazing campaign. The facts themselves will often give rise to the Big Idea which will sell the product.

It is the sweat and tears of research that gives rise to the creative inspiration. Smart advertisers and smart copywriters put this into practice. Back in the Mad Men days, companies would hire entry-level copywriters and use them in the first year or two to only do the research. They didn't even write a word of copy until after they mastered art of the researching.

Eugene Schwartz, the marketing legend, provides us with insight into creative salesmanship. Expanded on the value of research by explaining we should not only do research into the product but research our prospects as well. He came from humble beginnings and because of that was able to connect with every ordinary person.

He read the National Inquiry every week and watched the popular films that everybody was watching in order to write effective copy. You can't only read Tolstoy unless you really have made Russian History your niche. You must listen to Urber drivers, waitresses, shopkeepers, everyone you meet so you can become familiar with thei language they use and the kind of advertisement that appealed to them.

Research will also force you to do your math. I know all copywriters hate math. (I do too.) If we were any good at math we'd become engineers or accountants. But by applying mathematical models to the responses you get to tests of a new product you're about to release, you can predict sales. That can help you decide how much you can comfortably afford to spend to advertise it, based on the expected profits.

If the cost of advertising isn't justified by the potential profits, you might want to rethink your plans. David Ogilvy reported research indicating 60 percent of new products fail in test markets. Wouldn't it be better to know your product's chances of success through testing before rolling out an expensive campaign?

Research will help you compare yourself to your competition. By testing a new product, you plan to develop against the one your competition is already selling, you can see whether your version will be able to match the popularity of your competitor's product. You will also learn what you need to do to make your version more attractive.

Research will lead you to the best design. Package design plays a big role in the success of products. For example, the color of a package or the font used in a product name can make a huge difference in how appealing it is to potential buyers. Research can help you determine which design will get the most favorable attention and motivate people to buy.

Research will create your positioning. You can use research to determine how best to position your product. Maybe you've created a new snack food. Will you get the most sales by offering it as a yummy treat or a healthy one? Testing will help you discover which approach will appeal to the biggest audience.

Do you know who will want to buy your product? You would do well to determine your target audience before rolling out a big campaign. For example, you may think your product will appeal to twenty-somethings, and plan to advertise to that demographic, when in fact you should be targeting forty-somethings. Research could keep you from making a costly mistake.

Never rest on your laurels. You may have a successful product, but you must keep checking to see if consumers continue to see your product as desirable--and that requires research. If your image is slipping, you need to know about it.

David Ogilvy said that in many cases this happens when consumers notice you're using cheaper ingredients. Before you start making major changes to your formula, do research to find out whether it's noticeable, and if your customers find it objectionable.

Research will shine a light on your best benefits. Every great ad contains a promise. Ogilvy reported research showing that advertisements using headlines that promise a benefit are read by four times more people than advertisements without such headlines. Don't just give information in a headline: give a benefit.

Don't just say "One-Hour Dry Cleaning Service." Say "Get Ready on Short Notice with Our One-Hour Dry Cleaning Service." Or "Our One-Hour Dry Cleaning Service Makes You Look Like a Million Bucks."

Research will tell you if you have converted them from the competition. Ogilvy talked about pretesting television commercials, and his findings are applicable to any kind of promotion you may be doing. He said testing people's recall of commercials had no relation to their success at getting consumers to buy the product.

One of the more important issues, according to Ogilvy, was to test to see if your target audience has actually been converted away from your competitor in favor of your product?

He also said to keep testing ads for "wear-out." Eventually, even the best ad will lose its power because people's values change over time. Even if your ad is working, keep testing to see if its numbers continue to hold up. As soon as they start slipping, be ready with the next big campaign idea (that hopefully you've also been pretesting all along).

Research will tell you if they are reading and remembering. If people don't read or remember your ads, they can't be persuaded by them to take action. Do the research to make sure your ads are getting through.

Anyway, there are bound to be disagreements as people consider different aspects of an ad. Having research available can help you make the best decisions possible, backed by science.

Marketing isn't easy. Being successful at it doesn't come from making decisions based on opinions or "feelings." To get people to buy your product, you have to know what they're thinking, what they like, and what you have to do to get their interest, overcome their skepticism, and win their hearts. The only way to know these things for sure is by doing the research.

On Testing Your Ad

One of the most important aspects of any copywriter is the ability to A/B test their ads. This is also called split testing which is comparing two different versions of your copy to see which one performs better. A/B testing allows you to make the most out of your ad. While the cost of acquiring a viewer can be a huge cost of increasing your conversions.

Testing is the only way you know your promotions are working and the only way you can improve scientifically. Testing is the only way you can improve and stay ahead of your competition. Most companies that aren't familiar with marketing don't like the idea of testing since it and evidently involves some wasted effort and money. But you need to waste both in order to's stay on top of your industry. It is ridiculous to spend money on advertising just because the copy is clever what looks like it should work. Only he can do is test it and adjust.

The best way to do this is to split the advertisement right down the middle so you send 50% of your leads to one at and 50% to the other. If you are doing a mailer just make sure that you have the ability to track the difference ads with the different promo code or a different phone number for example.

Things you can test

- Headlines

- Subheadlines

- Paragraph texts

- Testimonials

- Call to action

- Links

- Images

Except nothing is true about advertisement and marketing until you have tested it. I have worked for a gym in Toronto trying to improve their SEO.

We thought this was a difficult task given the competition in a competitive market and the budget was slim. But we managed to get them on the first page of Google in three months. It was similar with a real estate agent in West Vancouver. I thought to get him on the first page of Google was impossible but after a couple of months there he was. I didn't believe it myself until I tested it several different ways.

Alternatively, there was this furniture store that spent several thousand dollars on SEO and it took them over a year to get on the first plate of Google. Almost any marketer would've put their money on the furniture company heading number one first but it was the opposite. Do not assume anything in marketing until you have tested it first.

As you test results of each ad, use what you learn to create and improve the current version and then test that ad against another, and so on. This way you can build upon your success and create better and better ads and measure their response accordingly.

In advertising many factors we don't understand come into play. That's why it's so important to test correct testing correct again build upon your knowledge and what you learn within the industry and be willing to shift it's not working. In the same sense do not be enraptured by marketing gurus who claim to have all the answers.

Every new ad is a test of what worked before currency check results to see the truth of what is working even if this means admitting you are wrong the willing to scrap some clever copy or a beautiful picture is painful especially when you have worked on it lovingly for so long but a good marketer always keeps their ego in check.

The most important thing is to from your mistakes don't repeat them. Try to keep your mistakes to a minimum of course but you will make them and don't feel disappointed if something doesn't work out. I know it can be hard especially when you're dealing with other people's money but don't be daunted by failure. It's only failure unless you give up as a famous saying goes.

On Studying the Data

You'll have to use the website analytical tools such as Google Analytics and find where your leads are dropping off. Use a heat map to see where customers are looking and scrolling. Most landing page software these days comes with a heat map option. If not there are many different options.

Copywriting can be about creative differences which is why it's always best to test scientifically whether your promotion is working or not. With this information, you can increase the success of your campaign and your fee that goes with it. The only way to test the success is to measure it.

Accept nothing in marketing or advertisement is true unless scientifically proven. What will work in one campaign won't necessarily work and another. Different industries will respond to different copy better just because you think you know the car industry doesn't mean that your ad will work 100% of the time. And what works in the car industry might not work in the furniture industry.

Even when you have an ad that works and is getting above average results you still want to test different ads. You should go with an 80/20 rule of thumb here. You always want to be constantly improving, there is never perfect.

John Kappel's is one of the most famous copywriters of all time and was a pioneer in applying scientific methods to advertising. He reported a case in which one mail order advertisement sold almost 20 times as much merchandise as another. Without testing, he would've never known just by looking at the ad which would have converted more.

No amount of arguing in a boardroom would have been able to figure that out. So just remember when you get caught in the heat of the moment, arguing between two ideas neither of them are valid until tested. You're just wasting your breath, fighting over your ego.

Ways You Can Test Your Ad

It's important to let any copyright pre-for a day or two. Most copywriters and writers in general fall into the trap of thinking whatever their Briton is either really amazing or really terrible. We pumped with enthusiasm or despair. The reality is usually somewhere in the middle. If you believe your copy for a day then you are able to see the mistakes you made newly. You're a different person and you are able to look objectively.

You can see where what you've written doesn't make sense grenades clarifying or where you can simplify. You can see if you're missing a call to action or if it doesn't slow correctly.

Ask somebody to read your ad copy aloud to you. Does this sound strange? Maybe you're thinking, "shouldn't you read your copy aloud to someone else?" But the problem with reading your copy to someone else is that you know your own copy, so you read it with the right emphasis, and you learn nothing from the process.

When someone else reads your copy out loud to you, cold, unfamiliar with the material, you can tell right away where the stumbling blocks are, where the person obviously misunderstands your unclear copy, and where sentences are awkward or too long.

Now use what you learn. If the person doesn't understand something, that means your target audience probably won't understand it either. So look at how you can change the copy. If the person stumbles over your wording, smooth it out. This is a very effective way to perfect a piece.

Test your ad with an interview. Now that you've perfected your ad to some degree, get other people's opinions of it. Caples suggested using actual prospects for the product. For example, show ads for dog food to dog owners.

Always give people a choice of which ad, headline, illustration, etc., they prefer. If you just show them your ad and ask them whether they like it, they'll probably say yes because they don't want to hurt your feelings. But if you show them two headlines and ask which one they like better, you'll get a more honest opinion.

However, be aware that opinion tests by themselves are not enough; they are only opinions. Caples said you should always back up opinion tests with sales tests.

Caples offered different types of sales tests, including looking at responses to mail order tests, testing the use of coupons, testing the value of following up coupons with calls by a sales representative, offering samples and free literature, using coupons vs. "hidden offers" that were described in the text but not made obvious by the addition of a coupon, and split testing.

By testing selected variables in ads against one another and measuring which produced the greatest response, Caples developed a scientific approach to creating effective ads.

Caples acknowledged that advertising could never be an exact science like chemistry. In a chemistry lab, you can have complete control over all the variables.

But in advertising, there are too many unknown variables, and they are always changing. For example, the news of the day could be bad and cast a shadow on every ad published on that particular day. You would never be able to anticipate that through pretesting.

That doesn't mean there aren't great advantages to running tests. While you can never predict with precision how an ad will do, you can quickly identify ads that don't work at all, compared to ads that work very well. And then you can keep improving on those ads that work well, to make them work even better.

On Creativity

Both Schwartz and Hobart offered very practical steps or writing sales material that would convert. Swarts said to focus and find out everything you can about the product you're selling. Gather information, read through it, arrange it, and let your subconscious do all the work and a great piece of sales copy will emerge. Will gather as much information as you can about the product or service

Collect all the information you can't even if it doesn't seem relevant. Go through everything see what will jump out at you.

I know I've said this before, but it's important enough to repeat. Find out as much as you can about the target audience

If you're writing for an established company then get them to refer for five of their ideal clients to you. Ask them why they chose that particular service or product to begin with. But don't just in their. You want to branch out to potential buyers find out what the differences between them and clients' current customer base.

Are you targeting entrepreneurs? Or people who work 9-to-5? Where can you find these people? Discover what interests them what are their problems and what are their pain points.

Your job as a copywriter is to communicate between your client and his target market. All the pieces are there in front of you just have to put them together like a puzzle.

How does one become creative? How does one get new ideas? How does one solve problems that are seemingly impossible? That you've worked on for weeks and thrown your hands up in despair?

Your conscious mind is your focus of attention. The conscious mind is absorbed with what you are paying attention to. For example, you're no absorbed with reading this book. Your conscious mind can only hold about seven memory bytes. That's pretty small, so you have to focus.

A great example is Mozart, one of the most creative men to ever live, who was writing symphonies at eight years old. The movie Amadeus shows his life very truthfully and how he wrote. He never ever rewrote. He never changed. He wrote his scores in pen and ink. He never changed a note of them. They were always perfect and the highlight of his genius of course, but that doesn't mean a thing.

There is a very famous story about how he did it. He composed at a billiard table. He would stand at the billiard table, and he would have a single white billiard ball. He would have a pen and an inkwell, and he would have the score. And he would take the white billiard ball in his left hand while he had the pen in the right hand and he would throw the white billiard ball out against the three cushions. And it would bounce off the three cushions. It's random, how it comes back, to a certain extent. It never comes back exactly at the same place, so he had to focus on the trajectory of the billiard ball until it came back.

When it came back here or here or here, he had to focus on that hand being at the exact right place. Meanwhile, while his conscious mind was over here, his unconscious mind slipped the note back to him and then he had the next note. Every note was a billiard ball traveling. Every note was a distraction. Every note was an addition. You've got to break out of that conscious prison to be unconsciously creative, which means to connect unconsciously things that haven't been consciously connected before.

Chapter Six:

On Email Marketing

**Email has an ability many channels don't: creating valuable,
personal touches – at scale."**

– David Newman

Email still is the most powerful tool that a copywriter and
perhaps any market has. Despite the fact that people complain about
spam and there are so many social media gurus out there email is still
the number one way to get engagement and things sold on the
Internet. More things are sold by email than any other method
including all social media platforms combined.

One time, I was working for a cannabis company that shall
remain nameless. We were selling cannabis online across Canada. At
the time it was a bit of the Wild, Wild West as the regulations had just
made cannabis legal. We were competing for the top spot on Google
– namely because besides there were precious little other ways we
could advertise. Facebook and Instagram would constantly block our
accounts from even posting organic content. We had to be very
careful with everything we did; in many cases, we couldn't link
anything back to the website for fear of being shut down.

Therefore, we had to rely on SEO and email marketing – and
even email marketing was tricky. We couldn't use any of the major
players like Mailchimp or Constant Contact. We ended up using a
sketchy service that was from Switzerland.

One Friday night, we learned that the website had been
hacked. Everything had been taken over. We couldn't log into the

website. We couldn't log into the email. We couldn't communicate with our customers.

The culprit? We thought it was the old web developer since the domain and the hosting was still in her name. She had never transferred them over to the owners and therefore had complete access to the website. It turned out that she was owed $5,000 that had been unpaid. The owners, of course, denied this.

We spent the weekend trying to unhack the website. It turned out that one of the employees still had access to the website. The web developer hadn't recognized her name as a user and therefore hadn't kicked her out.

We called her but the assistant refused to help us. We checked about an hour later and found the assistant had been kicked out as well.

We were beginning to suspect a mole. Perhaps the web designer and the assistant were working together to take over the website.

We contacted one of the owners who said that the web designer was refusing to cooperate. It seemed she was accepting all the e-transfers into her personal account, which, if she kept it up, would total around $80,000 a month – or until the customers realized they were being swindled. Not a bad profit.

The two owners didn't want to go to the police or get lawyers involved but at this point, they had little choice. At one point, there was talk about sending some men to try and intimidate the web designer into giving the website back.

But in the meantime, their customers had no idea that the website had been taken over. The only solution was to communicate with them through email marketing.

Thankfully we had downloaded a recent email list and so we opened up a new email marketing software since we didn't have access to the old one.

We launched a new website under a new domain and used email to try and convince our customers that we had been hacked and were now operating under a new name.

We knew that if we were to survive as a business that email was our only way. Through several emails, we managed to get $2,000 in sales in under a 48 period. Not bad for a new brand with no reputation.

This story is meant to illustrate, firstly, don't get involved in the weed business. It might be lucrative but there are still very shady characters involved. Secondly, that email marketing is a very powerful tool.

The trick with email marketing is to be different from your competition. Now everybody is giving away something for free in exchange for an email list and then blasting them with sales messages. Like any sale, you need to build trust and ensure that you're selling them the right product.

For many small business owners, bloggers and entrepreneurs managing the daily operations as a full time 24 seven job. You don't often think about the higher-level assets like brand and unique selling proposition. Juggling all of these responsibilities often causes inserting things to fall to the wayside like marketing or building your customer base.

With email marketing promoting your business and connecting with the audience becomes a whole lot easier and cost-effective way.

With the rise of social media many assume email is not as effective any more is joining tactics like telemarketing but that is far from the truth. It is still far one of the top ways of building relationships with customers and should be the keystone of your marketing efforts.

Just the other day I sent out a short email for a client about an award he'd won in a local newspaper. That one email generated over 200 leads (this is in the industry where each sale is worth at least a couple thousand dollars) and somebody from the BC business Magazine sought now is doing a profile on the client which will generate probably thousands leads if not more. I wouldn't be surprised if by the end of it that one email will have brought in a quarter of $1 million. Email marketing is the most cost-effective form of marketing out there.

According to Weber almost a third of consumers prefer to receive communication from brands via email 66% of consumers have made a purchase online as result of an email marketing campaign hundred and 38% more is spent by consumers receive emails offers those who don't.

Aside from opportunities to grow your business, email marketing can also help build a community of loyal customers. A great thing about email is it is in your control and not the consumers. Businesses have very little choice of when or if a customer visits your website. Sure you can send out links through social media or pay for advertisement but ultimately it's the customers" decision whether to click or not. With email you can send out promotions or information any time you like.

Email, however, is so much more than just another way to advertise your brand. It's a way to make real connections with those who truly interested in your business.

On Make A Strategy

Before you begin collecting email subscribers or importing them into your list you should first take some time to think about what your email marketing strategy is who your target market is and start identifying your expectations and goals.

On Setting Goals

As you think about what you hope to achieve through email marketing, it will be helpful to ask yourself:

- How do you want your emails to help your business?
- Do you want to increase sales for your product?
- Do you want to build relationships with subscribers?
- Who is the ideal subscriber for your email list?
- How will it fit with your overall marketing strategy?

While these goals may evolve over time, it is important to consider the purpose of your emails and set goals of both measurable and attainable.

If you are just starting out an email marketing campaign, you might want to focus your goal and groomed subscribers. If this is the case goal might look like the following:

I plan to collect thousand email subscribers over the next year by leveraging social media, Google advertising and tradeshows.

As you plan your tactics, continue to target the market you hope to reach. For example, business coaches with a focus on improving the revenue of small businesses.

On Getting Subscribers

Engaging a list of subscribers the key to the success of any email marketing campaign. It is not just how many subscribers you have, but it's more about the quality and engagement level of the people who you have on your list. You have to make sure you the right people who are interested in your brand and what you have to share with them.

To help you grow your list and attract quality email subscribers there are a few steps you need to follow and it all begins with the signup form.

Sign up forms can either be in the header, sidebar or as a popup box that displays once your customer has been on your website.

On Types of Forms

Static sign up form: The regular sign up form is a classic way for attracting website visitors to subscribe to your email list. These are static blocks that you can put on your homepage, in your sidebar, in the middle or at the end of a blog post or on a dedicated page for subscribing.

Pop up form: These are a high converting option and work really well at attracting new sign ups. A pop up form will appear over your web page, and give you a bit more real estate to convey your value. Most tools will let you set the time before the form pops up as well (we recommend 45 seconds, but be sure to test this to see what works best for your audience).

Notification bar form: A notification bar form sits at the top of your site or blog. Pop up forms can be disruptive for some audiences, and static sign up forms can get lost in the content. The notification bar form is a great way to promote your form on the top of a web page and ensure that new visitors are aware of your email list.

Slide-in form: A slide-in form can be less intrusive than a pop up, and is perfect for pages that have a lot of content. As a user scrolls down a page, a simple sign up form will slide onto the screen, usually from the lower right corner. This engagement typically hits the reader after they've already started reading the post and obtained value from your content.

On Email Headlines

You guess it – headlines are the most important part of your email. If you don't have a compelling headline then it doesn't matter how good the rest of your email is. We cover headlines in detail so we won't say much here, only that you want to avoid the spam filters so don't use works like 'free' 'deal' and 'marketing' and don't put them in all caps. I remember one time I was in charge of the email marketing for a sex therapist. Now you may think sex therapy would be pure gold for a copywriter, Now try to avoid the spam folders on that one!

What can you sell by email?

You can sell almost anything by email, sometimes even products worth tens of thousands of dollars. Another heard somebody so anything over the million-dollar mark but that doesn't mean it's not possible.

What is the right time to send your emails?

This is the eternal question debated by all email marketers and there isn't a simple answer. There are so many variables that it's impossible to say for sure.

On Entertainment Value

Your emails should have two things: High level of entertainment value and an action you want your readers to take. Your emails never should be boring. That is the biggest crime you can commit as a copywriter.

How do you turn a dry subject into an entertaining one? The best way is to tell a story. People always remember stories.

One of the best copywriters out there is Ben Settle. He talks a lot about info-tainment. It is a term that was once coined for the media and journalism but now includes the marketing sphere. Ben Settle isn't for everybody and he knows that. He speaks directly to a male audience. (He regularly talks about banging chicks and how he's always right.) But you have to give him one thing – you remember what he says.

Why do you need info-tainment? Because we are constantly bartered by so many different marketing messages (sometimes tens of thousands in a day) and we have so many choices, we need to have a reason why the potential customer will open your email rather than the hundreds of other things they can be doing.

You can't just write: 'Buy my product, buy my product." Your emails need to be fun and lighthearted. (Unless of course, you are raising funds for refugees or cancer survivors.) Don't be afraid to add a little spark to your emails to make them memorable.

On The Open Loop

The open look email is like a serial television show. You tell a story but end each email with a cliffhanger just like Game of Thrones or Breaking Bad. Then you watch the next episode and sure enough, it also ends with a cliffhanger and before you know it your entire day is gone. It's no wonder binge-watching has become so prevalent.

What is it about these shows that make them so addictive? And how good would it be if we could apply those same techniques in your marketing and emails so people would be begging you to send them more emails?

The open-loop technique is a copywriting tactic where you open a story in your copy and take several emails to close it with a satisfactory ending. It works because our brains are hard-wired for stories. There are numerous studies that show we remember things better in story format. That's why fables were created, to drill in those lessons to those kids.

We feel anxious when there is a gap between what we know and what we don't, and so we are compelled to seek out the missing information to reduce the anxiety we feel.

On How To Use Open Loops

By using open-loop techniques in your subject lines and by effective storytelling, you can create that gap of information that compels people to open your email to learn more and effectively close the loop.

The key to making this work lies in figuring out what your reader wants to know. Think about this for a moment. Chances are you probably don't particularly care what the originals of the term "piggy bank" comes from. You're not about to stop what you're reading and Google it.

Before you start incorporating this technique into your own emails, remember there is masses of information people don't know and are an open loop and an open loop only works in your subject lines and emails if your reader wants to know the information. It has to be relevant and desirable and make them want the information.

Here is a brilliant example of an open loop. This radio ad was written for a diamond seller named Woody Justice by the Wizard of Ads himself, Roy H. Williams, but could have just have easily been in an email format.

Antwerp, Belgium, is no longer the diamond capital of the world.

Thirty-four hours on an airplane. One way. Thirty. Four. Hours. That's how long it took me to get to where eighty percent of the world's diamonds are now being cut. After 34 hours I looked bad. I smelled bad. I wanted to go to sleep. But then I saw the diamonds.

Unbelievable. They told me I was the first retailer from North America ever to be in that office. Only the biggest wholesalers are allowed through those doors. Fortunately, I had one of 'em with me, a lifelong friend who was doing me a favor.

Now pay attention, because what I'm about to say is really important: As of this moment, Justice Jewelers has the lowest diamond prices in America, and I'm including all the online diamond sellers in that statement.

Now you and I both know that talk is cheap. So put it to the test. Go online. Find your best deal. Not only will Justice Jewelers give you a better diamond, we'll give you a better price, as well.

I'm Woody Justice, and I'm working really, really hard to be your jeweler. Thirty-four hours of hard travel, one way. I think you'll be glad I did it.

The ad starts off by setting up an open loop: if Antwerp is no longer the diamond cutting capital of the world, which city is?

But we're not told which city. We're strung along with the hint that it takes a 34-hour plane trip to get there. The listener's curiosity starts to intensify. He wants to know where this mysterious place might be.

Then we're told that to be allowed into this inner sanctum of diamond buyers — a place out of reach to every other retailer in America — is to have access to prices lower than the competition can match. How much lower remains an open question, and so another loop is opened in the mind of the listener.

Finally, the ad closes by circling back to the 34-hour trip without ever closing, or in Hollywood terms called the payoff, either the "how much lower" or the "which city was it" loops.

Now the itch to find out "where'd you fly to, Woody?" or to see just how great the prices are — well, those are the obvious parts of the ad, the ones everyone recognizes on a first listen.

Don't Over Do Open Loops

I'm sure you've seen stories on social media that go something like this:

"She was pronounced brain dead, but what happened next will shock you!"

Now, this technique is so popular is because it works. (Remember John Caples headline: They laughed when I sat down at the piano but when I began to play.) But it's also very overused and thus people are now becoming immune to it and even make fun of it.

Similarly, you may also want to consider the effect this technique will have on your brand. What once was a popular technique now becomes clickbait and cheesy. Of course, if you're OK Magazine and that's what you're going for then by all means. . . Just know your audience and who you're targeting.

On Follow Up Emails

What makes the difference between a good response rate and a bad response rate? Follow up and hitting them with multiple methods of outreach.

Don' take it personally that people don't click on your link or even open your first email; they're either busy, don't have time or simply didn't see it.

In fact, most responses don't come on the first, second, third or even fourth email. They come on the sixth, seventh and eighth. Persistence is the key.

This means that one email is likely not going to do the trick and that you will need to follow up with prospects over a period of weeks or days and have *at least* 4 follow up emails. You might feel as if you're hounding them but if you do it in a respectful way and with good intentions then your prospect won't get annoyed.

And while we're on the subject, please don't use any of the following email subject headlines in your follow ups:

- "Just following up"
- "Touching base"
- "About my proposal
- "Did you receive my last email?"

And any variation of those. Why? Because they add no value. In the short attention span of your buyers, if your first sentence is "Did you receive my last email?" you've wasted valuable real estate where you can hit them with a different value.

So what works? Simply email them with a different approach.

For example, a follow-up email would be phrased:

```
Hey Bill,

I forgot to mention that another thing hiring
a copywriter will do is use email marketing
to increase your overall sales. I know you're
busy but if you click on the link, you can
find out more about how email marketing can
streamline your business.
The email doesn't even touch on the fact that
you emailed them before, you're not coming
across as desperate and you're giving them
another pitch on a different angle.
```

On Autoresponders

The autoresponder is your best friend as a marketer. It really is the simplest, most cost-effective way of keeping your customers engaged.

If you don't know what an autoresponder is, it sends a time sequence of emails to anyone who subscribes to your list. It could be sent every day, every week, or once a month. You can determine the frequency I can even make it to specific days after the initial follow-ups. It's pretty programs and planned is delivered automatically to every person in your email list or a segment of it. This is incredibly powerful especially if you're using a sequence to introduce people to you, your company, and your services and let them know through a series of storytelling or informative emails.

The autoresponder should be a welcome message a prospect receives when he or she signed up for a mailing list. Perhaps the mocha message delivered is a free report, a white paper or a gift of some kind explaining what to expect in your emails.

On Why Use Autoresponders:

- They let you continually showcase your best content
- Deliver the same high-value experience to every new subscriber.
- Are great places to mention relevant offers
- Allow you to build trust with your audience slowly and ensure your new subscribers don't forget you.

On What Should You Write In Your Autoresponders?

Your autoresponders, like all your other emails, should offer your subscribers something of value. Maybe it's training or advice about their market. The more value you provide your subscribers, the more they will be addicted to your email.

You could share your story. Tell the readers how you started your business, what struggles you went through and how you succeeded. The danger here is that you can't make it all about yourself. The lessons and morals must be inspirational and you must key learnings.

You could provide a resource list. This can be blogs, books, videos, podcasts and other online tools. People love to have shortcuts and if you can curate all the information for them your subscribers will be happy.

Provide a case study. You got a compelling story about the success of a client who is going clear measurable results from your products or services write the story in a short case study. The short case they should include advice your subscribers can implement.

Here are some other suggestions for autoresponders:

1. Become an amazing teacher. Your emails don't have to be lengthy, brilliant, or fancy, but they do need to be useful to your subscriber. If possible, teach your subscriber something in every autoresponder message you send.

2. Give subscribers what you promised. If you say you'll give new subscribers a free report, case study, or video, provide an easy-to-use download link so they can instantly get their free gift.

3. Add some personality to your messages. Autoresponders shouldn't be boring. Spice them up by using your own voice and personality in your message. Be funny, quirky, and interesting — as long as it fits your brand.

4. Help your audience get to know and trust you. With each message, reveal a little glimpse into who you are and what you stand for.

5. Open a two-way conversation. Invite your subscribers to respond to your emails or join the discussion in a Facebook group or website. Ongoing discussion can help turn your subscribers into your biggest advocates.

6. Share other ways to connect with you. If someone joins your email list, it's likely he or she will want to connect with you on his or her favorite social media platform, too. Again, a Facebook group is a great way to build a tribe.

7. Keep adding and improving to it over time. Your autoresponder series should be a living "document," so review, edit, and add to it over time. Always get feedback from you customers an tweak it as necessary. Confirm that your messages are still relevant and useful.

8. Plan out the entire sequence before you start writing. Write a quick outline of how many messages you want to include and how far apart those messages will be delivered. Your outline will keep you on track as you write the whole sequence.

On Planning and Creating your Autoresponders

How many autoresponder emails should you have? A good guide is between three and five to start. But you can always add more you want.

The email should come close enough together that you engage your subscriber far enough apart that they don't annoy them. It is always a fine balance and there are no right or wrong answers.

What I would suggest is this: The welcome email should, of course, come as soon as he subscriber signs up. The second email should come between two and five days later. The third bout a week after that.

1. Plan how many autoresponder emails you want in your series (starting with three-to-five emails is a good guideline).
2. Decide how far apart each email will be sent.
3. Dedicate time to writing the whole series.
4. Queue them up in your email service provider.
5. Test the series to make sure everything works properly.

Once you've finished those steps, you can drive visitors toward your opt-in form and start getting sign-ups.

Then you can breathe easy, knowing your opt-in form is automatically handling an important part of your marketing for you.

And little by little, subscriber by subscriber, you'll be on your way to building a strong and long-lasting relationship with the members of your list.

On Newsletter Giveaways

People will opt because they want something of value from you. People won't give you their email address just to get another newsletter from you. You must offer them a compelling reason for the month to sign up to your mailing list. This can be a special report or a video course. Make sure it is in line with the type of person you are attracting. For example, if you want to use teach people on copywriting that you're not going to offer them a report on graphic design.

It's getting harder to add value to people's lives because the digital space is just getting so much more crowded. You need to be creative with the type of giveaway you have. You obviously can't afford to give away the farm but perhaps you could ship them a free copy of your favourite book or maybe an hour free consultation. These are just suggestions from the top of my head. You know yourself and your audience best. Put your noggin to good use and come up with something that people will say "I got to have that!"

Chapter Seven:

On Headlines

On the average, five times as many people read the headline as read the body copy. When you have written your headline, you have spent eighty cents out of your dollar.

—David Ogilvy

Headlines are the most important aspect of any ad copy. Most copywriters agree that an amateur copywriter with a good headline will outsell a legendary copywriter with a mediocre headline. Headlines are your first and perhaps your only impression you get to hook your potential customer.

You should spend most of your time writing copy thinking of headlines. Gary Halbert says that 80% of success is because of the headline. It is wet is going to cut through the surrounding noise and get people to pay attention.

Advertising legend Claude Hopkins reported that he had seen 8 to 10 times increased result just by making a small adjustment to a headline. That is why we should always be A/B testing new headlines out to see if they get better results.

I was working for this nude art gallery, trying to promote an event they were hosting in Toronto. Now you might think that you don't need a headline when it comes to nude art. Just show people a picture of a naked body and they'll instantly become interested in the event.

The problem was that much of our promotion was through social media and most of these platforms don't allow nudity. I learned this the hard way as I tried to bend the rules. In fact, I got blocked from Facebook for 60 days when I tested the limits. As a copywriter, trust me, it makes your life very difficult (and embarrassing as I told my other clients that I couldn't create their Facebook ad).

Thankfully my good copywriting skills came in handy as I was able to promote the event with words instead of pictures. In the end, we were able to drive people to the event using great headlines, text and exclusive interviews with the photographers and artists.

Headlines are now more important than ever before because they break through the clutter that's on the internet. It's so easy to get distracted or can we want to something else though your headline must grab the reader's attention right away. This includes email subject lines, social media, and even chapter titles.

What is the Purpose of the Headline?

Legendary copywriter Eugene Schwartz said the purpose of the headline is not to sell but rather to capture attention. This may seem counterintuitive to a lot of what people have taught. As you read through logs mail order social media you have about five seconds to catch the reader's interest. People decide on whether to keep reading in those few seconds.

The headline's only purpose is to get people to read the rest of the copy. It doesn't sell a product. Without a headline that turns A skimming reader into an interested prospect, the rest are words are useless. A great headline can communicate a full message to its intended audience and must lure the reader into the rest of the text. Compelling headlines must promise some soda benefit or reward for the reader and trade for the valuable time he or she is giving you.

According to legendary copywriter Robert Bly there are eight types of headlines that help you sell more.

A direct headline goes straight to the heart. Simple, straightforward and obvious benefit. An example would be $50 off your next appointment.

And indirect headline takes a more subtle approach uses curiosity to raise questions in the reader's mind the body copy answers. It can often have a double meaning. For example, how to lose 30 pounds in 30 days.

And use headline ask some aspect of venues and turns it into sales copy. Take something new or revolutionary about your product puts it in the headline. What my interview with Warren Buffett taught me about investing.

How to headline is extremely popular these days you see them and blog posts everywhere. The word how is extremely powerful and copywriting. According to Bly he stated it's impossible to write a bad line when you start with the word how. As a reason for how headline works all that's because people read to be informed about a certain topic.

A question headline is equally as powerful and almost used as often as to how headline. An example of this headline would be do you know the secrets that top 1 percent wealthiest people know? A question headline must do more than simply ask a question it must sympathize with the reader who would like the question answered.

The command headline tells the prospect what you need to do that should have strong verb demanding action such as subscribe today. Don't miss out on this amazing offer!

The reason headline which should have a number of product features tips which can be incorporated into the headline. An example of this would be ten tips to become a better writer.

Lastly, there's the testimonial headline which is extremely effective because it presents an outside proof that what you offer has great value. It is the most important type of marketing. You have to take what somebody says about you or your product and service and use actual words in your headline. An example of this would be I read the Wall Street Journal every morning.

How Do You Write your Headlines?

Eugene Schwartz again had the answer to this question. He was one of the hardest working copywriters ever to live. He did copious amounts of research before putting a single word to the page. You have to research everything you can about the product. Sometimes it will be to put to separate ideas together into something new and wonderful.

Gary Halpert came up with this formula he named AIDA. First, you have to catch their attention; second, you have to capture the interest, third, you have to create desire; and, forth you got to motivate them to action. In otherwords:

Attention

Interest

Desire

Action

Your headline should be memorable and should create curiosity in the reader.

Again you'll want to come up with five headlines you think are winners and test them with real audiences. Don't do a group test within the company as I've seen so many copywriters do. Let the results speak for themselves.

Every copywriter, blogger and journalist knows the importance of powerful headlines. Spent that many still under estimates the power of headlines and therefore don't take as much time to craft an excellent one. Amateur copywriter will start with the

the body and hone and craft that and then come up with the headline to match it.

The master copywriter starts with the headlines comes up with 10 to 20 examples and then works on the body. He or she will then go back to the headline perhaps come up with some more headlines but also eliminating the ones that don't work. You should spend at least 50% of your time working on your headline, perhaps even more. If you have great body text but not a great headline no one will get to the text.

Eugene Swarts often spent an entire week on the first 50 words of a sales piece. (The opening headline and first paragraph.) According to Copyblogger, eight out of 10 people read your headline but only 2 out of 10 will read your body text. That is why it's so important to have an amazing headline so people will continue on reading. While a great headline doesn't guarantee you success the benefits conveyed in the headline still need to be properly satisfied in the body copy.

Think of what the reader will get out of reading the text. What specifics can you add to make the headline more believable? Nobody believes the nine out of 10 scientists say anymore. Using exact figures subconsciously makes it more believable. Is your headline trigger strong emotion that encourages the reader to delve deeper?

They Laughed When I Sat Down At the Piano But When I Started to Play!

This is one of the most powerful and famous headlines ever written. This headline is so incredibly powerful because it taps into our motion that some point rather and our life have all been laughed at and ridiculed. Other important thing is that as you can see the writer overcame the fear of being laughed at and even showed them who was boss.

Copywriting trainers at American Writers & Artists teach The Four U's approach to writing headlines. Headlines, subheads and bullets should:

- Be USEFUL to the reader,

- Provide him with a sense of URGENCY,

- Convey the idea that the main benefit is somehow UNIQUE,

- Do all of the above in an ULTRA-SPECIFIC way.

Copywriter Clayton Makepeace says to ask yourself seven questions before you start to write your headline:

1. Does the headline reward the reader?

2. Does it create curiosity?

3. What specifics would you add to make your headline more intriguing and desirable?

4. Does your headline trigger a strong emotional response? Does it inspire the reader to take action?

5. Does your headline present a proposition that will instantly get your prospect nodding his or her head?

6. Could your headline benefit from the inclusion of a proposed transaction?

7. Could you add an element of intrigue to drive the prospect into your opening copy?

Makepeace's seven questions combined with the basic structure of The Four U's provide an excellent framework for writing spectacular headlines.

On Subheadlines

Subheadlines are important because your reader is going to first scan the copy and these are useful to break it up and make it easily digestible. How many subheadlines depends on how long your text should be. You should have no more than three paragraphs before you break it up with a subheadline.

Remember that subheadlines should follow the same principle as your main headline. Test it using the AIDA principle.

How long Should your Headlines Be?

There's no universal agreement on how long headline should be. Short headlines have been as successful as long headlines. Barack Obama and his 2008 presidential campaign was extremely successful with the one-word headline from an email. It read "Hey". In fact this is a brilliant headline from a presidential candidate. First off it's different from any other email subject line you have ever read before. It sticks out because it is so short. Of the reason it was successful was because it was casual. Presidents are supposed to be formal and authoritative but Obama appeared as an ordinary citizen. (Trump is definitely an ordinary citizen but that's a whole nother topic altogether.)

On Personalization

If at all possible you want to personalize your headline and copy. This is the ultimate attention grabber. It's like somebody calling out your name in a crowded supermarket. You will always look up and see who is calling out to you.

People always gravitate towards something that has been personalized exactly to them. This is easily done if you have a database with their names and emails. Almost all email marketing software allows you to create a tag that will automatically enter their name into the subject headline.

The secret way to lose 20 pounds in just five days!

Most likely the copywriter is trying to sell some sort of herb or vitamins. When the reader realizes that it really isn't this huge secret and they become cynical of copywriters and trust them less because of it. Do not lie or exaggerate in your copy whatever the circumstance is.

It will be tempting. People naturally gravitate towards secrets and huge claims and you'll see you click-through rate jump — at least at first. But when your readers find out that your claims aren't true it will hurt your brand and ultimately yourself.

Let's look at Gary Halpert's headline. This headline has everything you could possibly want in a headline.

At Last! Scientists Discover New Way To Look Younger In Just 17-Days!

"At last!" suggests something new and exciting, something that the reader has been waiting for.

Using scientists suggests authority and the fact that it has been clinically tested. (Again don't you scientists unless it actually has been tested by scientists. The reader will soon learn the truth especially when everything is easily Googled)

Discover again means that its new and that no one else has this method. To look younger is a benefit that we all want. I mean who doesn't want to look younger? In 17 days suggest that it's that easy solution and who doesn't want something that's quick and simple

Claude Hopkins said it, "Generalities fall off your readers like water off a duck's back." The specificity of 17 days makes our headline more believable, more easily understood and somehow, more interesting and, more real.

You should spend a lot of time reading and writing lines. Look at these papers magazines and other sales copy for inspiration. You should always have a swipe file on hand to put interesting clippings away. When you're at the checkout counter in the supermarket checkout's the magazines and how they write headlines. You should especially pay attention to trashy magazines as they write something best headlines in the world.

Good headlines are crucial. As much as it pains me to say this, *Enquirer* and other gossip magazines are written well enough to catch and hold your attention. They are clear, concise, crisp and, sadly enough, the most easily understood articles of any publication.

And what do *Enquirer* writers excel at above all else? You guessed it because we've been over this before, <u>HEADLINES</u>. Their headlines are so powerful, they have so much "grabbing power" that, every week, people who have sworn they'll never again buy such a publication, are almost forced to purchase it in spite of themselves.

If the best way to get good at writing is by writing, what is the best way to get good at writing headlines?

By the way, all this seems to be working out so well I think we're going to "syndicate" our advertising by making our collective expertise available to one other furniture dealer in each metro area throughout the U.

OK, as promised a few pages ago, I am now going to reveal the simple way to "massage" all this data to come up with something new. First, I do what I just did. Namely, I review what's already been done. Next, I get to my own personal collection of "headline cards" and pick them up and fondle them (I'm getting excited!) and look at them and think about them and flip them out onto the floor like I would a deck of cards and I cogitate and I remember..

Someone once said that freedom of speech does not give you the right to yell "Fire!" in a crowded theater. Remember your headline must not only grab attention, it must also be true and relevant.

**The Amazing Secret Of The Local
Jewellery Designer Who Is Giving
Away All Those Free Samples!**

This type of headline used to be very popular but now customers can see right through it. Don't use "Amazing Secrets" unless they really are truly amazing. (Ninety-nine percent of the time they aren't.) And what type of jewellery designer gives away free samples? Customers are so accustomed to sales messages they can sniff out a fraud when they see one. You need to build trust and credibility in your headlines.

And here is another one of my pet peeves:

Wasn't That A Nifty Way To Kill Two Birds With One Stone?

Quit being so clever! Look, I get it. You wouldn't be a writer if you didn't have secret love similes, hyperboles, and clever wordplay. Puns and in-jokes and linguistic play are the writer's delight. Just realize they may not be your audience's delight. Deep down we *all* want to be Shakespeare.

The writers *craft* is a good thing. Thinking carefully about language will make it clearer and more powerful, and that's what you want. But great copywriters know that cleverness too often leads directly to audience confusion.

A dash of cleverness here and there can add seasoning, so if you do use it, use it sparingly — and never in a headline.

Now this ad has all the elements of effective copy and it would take hours to explain every little detail so I'm going to cover the big takeaways and explain how to use these ideas to make massive improvements to your own copy.

Let's start with the most important piece of copy which is always your headline.

1. All standard copywriting courses teach you to call out your prospects in the headline and in this case, the target audience is

bankruptcy attorneys. Make sure the headline lets prospects know the copy is talking about people just like them.

If your customers are divorced people say something in the headline which makes them think "hey that's me!"

2. Never give away the secret or lead on that what they are about to read is an ad. Make your headline sound like a news story just as Nader did in this case.

3. Make sure your prospects can see from the headline there may be some benefit by reading the ad. The bankruptcy lawyers reading this ad are obviously hoping to learn how people like them are cashing in on new bankruptcy laws.

4. Make sure your headline talks about something which appears to be happening now. All humans have a fight or flight response to anything new. That is to say they immediately try to determine if this is something they want to get away from or if this is something they want.

You can trigger the response which makes them feel like they need to run after your products by wording the headline in such a way that something good for them is happening right NOW as opposed to about to happen or has happened.

Here is an example:

Compare these two headlines...

Copywriters Who Took The Halbert Workshop In The Past Have Been Able To Double Their Prices

or

Copywriters Signing Up For The New Halbert Workshop Are Able To Double Their Prices!

Which headline grabs you more? Do you care about what happened in the past? The Ipod used to be the hottest product on the market but now nobody would be caught dead with one. You need to convey this is important right now!

To end this chapter here are some of my alltime favourite headlines to get your creative juices flowing.

A Beer With More Substance Than A Hipster's Handmade Leather Journal

> \- Garagista Beer

It's Like A First Date Without the Awkward Silence

> \- Harley Davidson

Outrun Your Voice Mail

> \- Infinity

Admit it. You've Always Been Crazy About Topless Models

> \- Mahindra Classic

Men Talk About Women, sports, and Cars. Women Talk About Men Inside Sports Cars.

> \- Mercedes

Honestly now, did you spend your youth dreaming about someday owning a Nissan or Mitsubishi

> \- Porsche

It Makes Your House Look Bigger

- Volkswagen

Picks Up Five Times More Women Than A Lamborghini

- Daihatsu

They Don't Write Songs About Volvos

- Corvette

Of Course There's a Return On Your Investment. We Just Can't Print it Here.

-De Beers

Just Do it.

-Nike

Absolute Power Corrupts. Enjoy

-Apple

Protected By More Prenups Than Any Other Car

-Aston Martin

Maybe She's Born with it. Maybe it's Maybelline

-Maybelline

Chapter Eight:

On Website Copy

Copy is a direct conversation with the consumer.
- Shirley Polykoff

Do you need a website for your business? The answer is almost always yes. If you a business that relies on networking and referrals, like a financial planner, an accountant, it's possible to get away without a website. Maybe. But now almost everybody goes online to make some sort of purchasing decision, whether it's to do research or to actually buy online. Therefore your website is one of your primary marketing tools.

Your website should be more than just a pretty face of your company. It should entice your customers to take action. The terrible copy I find on web sites is atrocious. Most website designers don't even bother with the copy. They eat there just put terrible placeholder text or they rely on the client to provide. This is a terrible practice. I would say 95% of websites have terrible copy. They speak way too much about their own company and not enough about the benefits to the customer.

Part of the problem is that with globalization too many companies are getting their websites created in India or China or somewhere else that doesn't speak English as a first language. These companies have no respect for the words you place on your website. Now there's nothing wrong with hiring a company from another country but need to hire an experienced copywriter to finish the job.

Website copy often doesn't speak to the consumer because it's too busy talking about how great the company is. However the consumer doesn't care about your company or about you and only cares about what you can do to make their life better happier and simpler.

Website design is know nothing about creating sales or how to inspire action. They worry on the latest animation graphic design and colour scheme. Now there's nothing wrong with having any of that but if it doesn't to anything for your bottom line than just a waste of money. I know you might say that it all goes the brand and the authority of the company which is true but if somebody doesn't come to your website and immediately want to subscribe to your email list or some other action, then you are doing it.

I like Gary Halbert's definition of HITS. "How idiots track success". If you have 100,000 hits but no sales then something is off with your website.

When a potential customer comes to your website there will be looking for information about your product. Make sure that it is accessible and easy to find. Doesn't need to be in a written format but potentially video or even audio sometimes.

So now you what I website shouldn't be we will go through the various pages and I will show you what copy should be on each one.

On Home Pages

You should have your main headline across the banner of your website. This should not be something about your company instead should be the main benefit the customer will get if they hire you or buy your product. Too many times I see:

"XYZ Company is the best at manufacturing pens."

You customers don't care that you claim to be the best at manufacturing patents. They only care about themselves and what your product can do for them and how it is beneficial.

A better headline would be:

"The most reliable and smooth writing utensil for everyday use."

If you want more instructions on how to write amazing headlines go to the headline chapter.

Again most homepages will go on to explain about the company's history or what the company does instead of trying to sell the reader on the product. All that for the about page which is generally the seconds most visited page after the home page.

On About Pages

This page is a chance for you to stand out above your competition. You should think about what makes you unique. Don't write some lame, boring copy that makes your prospect fall asleep. Yes your history and experience is relevant but don't make it the main point just to fill the page.

In this page you should have your guarantee. This is something that you promise to your customers all the time. Whether it is on-time delivery, the best price, or the best customer service, make sure that this is clearly stated on this page.

You also need your "why" on this page. Why do you do what you do? Most businesses don't have a strong "why". They just fell into what they are doing by accident or thought it would be a good way to make money. The 'why' is why you are passionate about what you do. It is more than a mission statement. In fact, don't write anything as boring as a mission statement on your about page. The 'why' should be a part of everything you do

The best brands in the world like "Apple", "Virgin" "Starbucks," and "Southwest" airlines know why they are doing what they are doing. It's not simply to make a better computer, a foamy latte or get you from point 'A' to point 'B'. They want to improve the world and disrupt the status quo. If you have a strong 'why' then you don't just have customers, you have fans. These fans won't just buy your product, they will buy into your philosophy. They will be ambassadors of your brand. They will rave about you to their friends; they will rave about you to their family.

This is also the one place where I would encourage you to have a professionally done photograph. You appear a lot more trustworthy if your customer can actually see what you look like. A lot of people don't like to have their photo on their website but your customers connect with photographs. It's the next best thing to talking to them in person.

On Testimonials

Testimonials and case studies are the third most important page on your website. Everybody knows that word of mouth marketing is the most powerful simply because it's not you tooting your own horn but rather a third party confirming your abilities.

This creates a huge trust factor and shows the customer that you are able to deliver on your promises.

So what does a testimonial consist of?

Here we go back to Aristotle and to the three act structure of any good storyteller. It is simple and straightforward yet sometimes isn't followed.

It should start what was the problem the customer was facing. Maybe they'd didn't have enough clients or maybe they weren't sure what their target market was or how they should advertise. This should address any objections your client had in hiring you. If your service is expensive here is where you want to explain why hiring somebody that is less expensive would actually be detrimental to the client.

The second component is how you helped them and what you did. Explain in simple and straightforward detail of the steps you took to solve your customer's problem.

The third component should be what the results were of your work and why the customer was happy. You want to be as specific as possible. Sometimes the customer won't let you release the actual data but you can say something along the lines of increased customer sales by 40% then this is where you want to write it down.

On Video

A video testimonial is even more powerful than a written one. Explain to your customer the above formula before they go on camera and you'll get an extremely powerful testimonial.

If you're like me, you're hard-pressed to buy anything without reading comments on Amazon. We want to know we're making the right decision, and what could be sincerer than the endorsement of third party assessment of people who have already bought and used the product?

While marketers have sold things using customer testimonials since - well probably the beginning of time - the use of such opinions has ballooned in recent years with internet reviews. It's easier now more than ever before to whip out our cellphones and Google reviews. We go online to read what everyday people have to say about restaurants, movies, and the products at Best Buy.

A recent poll conducted by Real Estate Business Online in 2013 found that 73.5 percent of their real estate professional respondents believe that testimonials are essential to building their businesses.

One of the reasons testimonials can be more effective than you simply talking up your own business is that they seem more authentic, and therefore trustworthy.

If you say how great your own product is, it sounds like bragging. And of course, you have an ulterior motive to make yourself sound as good as possible. But if some disinterested third party says how great your product or service is, it's more believable.

If prospects know nothing about you, they require a good deal of selling on your part to convince them that you deserve their business. Testimonials can be an important part of that sales process by making prospects feel more at home with you. They feel they know you better because of what others say about you.

The testimonials help you take a short cut into your prospects' good graces. So, if you have testimonials from happy customers, you should, by all means, use them.

What Makes a Great Testimonial?

It's not as simple as slapping together some nice words about your product. When choosing which testimonials to help sell your product, here are some things you need to look for.

1. The testimonials need to appear credible. If people think that you made up the testimonial yourself, it will dampen response instead of increasing it.

2. It can't be over-hyped. It can't sound too slick, like it was written by a used car salesman.

3. The more specific the testimonial is, the better. Just saying something was good is not going to help you.

4. Personal stories of the individual's experience with the product or service are especially nice. And enthusiastic reviews are much more effective than lukewarm statements.

    The more information you can give about the person giving the testimonial, the better. First name, last name, and city and state would be ideal. First name and last initial, along with city and state is standard. And while we're at it, don't publish any testimonial or place it online without written permission.

5.   People are always drawn to pictures, so if the person writing the testimonial is willing to provide you with one, try to use it.

6.   It's nice to have a series of testimonials from a variety of types that cover the range of your customer base, for example, both men and women if that's appropriate for your product.

     You want to make sure your testimonials come from your target audience. If you primarily sell to senior citizens, that's who your testimonials should come from. And if they can directly speak to concerns of senior citizens they will be especially effective.

     "As a woman in my seventies, I was hesitant to have a construction crew come to my home. But the people at Acme Construction were wonderful. And they refitted my bathroom with a walk-in tub and grab bars so that I feel comfortable in my own home again."

7.   Don't tell them that's all you've got. You want to give the impression that this is just a sampling of the many testimonials you have on file from satisfied customers (For example, "Here are just some of the glowing comments we received from satisfied customers over the past year.")

8.   Finally, a great testimonial sounds authentic. Similar to #1, if your testimonials sound fake or canned, they're going to work against you instead of working for you.

     That means the language may be a little confused, or the story line a bit jumbled. You may be tempted to polish it up, but don't do too much, if anything all. If a word is obviously misspelled you can fix it. But don't rewrite testimonials to make them sound better. They will be more effective if they sound genuine.

How Do You Get Testimonials?

If one of your clients or customers spontaneously sends you a testimonial, that's great. But even if someone loves your product or service, they won't necessarily think to provide you with a testimonial.

So, if you're talking to a customer who praises your work, go ahead and ask if they would be willing to write down their comments and let you use them in some of your marketing materials.

You may be surprised at how many people will say yes, as long as you promise not to provide any more identifying information about them than they feel comfortable revealing.

Keep hard copies of written testimonials. Also, get written permission to use the testimonials, and keep it on file. Hang on to those permission slips, even after you stop using that particular testimonial. It should be a permanent file.

How Do You Use Testimonials?

Use testimonials in all your written sales materials. If you have video testimonials, put them on your website, and extract quotes to use in your written materials.

Use a variety of testimonials from different customers and clients, and keep updating their use. If you use the same testimonial for 20 years, it may look as though that's the only testimonial you ever received.

If it's a great one, it may become part of your company image. But in general, the more testimonials you have, and the more you change them out, the more it looks like you're a growing company that is continuing to get new satisfied customers.

Testimonials are a powerful selling tool that can help ease the doubts of new prospects. If you have testimonials, use them. If you need more testimonials, ask for them. A satisfied customer may prove to be your most effective marketer.

Chapter Nine:

On Salesy Copy

I do not regard advertising as entertainment or an art form, but as a medium of information. When I write an advertisement, I don't want you to tell me that you find it 'creative.' I want you to find it so interesting that you buy the product.

-David Ogilvy

Sales is the most valuable skill you can learn, and yet it's taught in very few places. I'm not sure why very few people teach sales. It's certainly something you don't get taught in school. You can listen to audiobooks but unless you go out and practice it you'll never get good at it.

When I mean sales it really is the art of enrollment and persuasion. If you want any success in life, if you want to become independently wealthy all you need to do is get good at sales. This one technique is the answer to all your problems. If you can become a good salesperson then you never have to worry ever again. Wouldn't that be great? You may think that's ridiculous. Never worry again. But if you became a great salesperson then you would be able to persuade and enroll anybody. It can be as small as enrolling your friends to go see that movie you want and as big as persuading that person you love to marry you. It could be getting your kids to clean their room or could be getting a new job or promotion.

Copywriting really is just salesmanship in print. No other skill comes even close to this.

The most important aspect of a salesperson is their mindset. You learned all about mindset in chapter 2 so I won't go over this again but you'll need these s skills to become masterful in selling anything.

First, you need to sell yourself before you can sell anybody else. Eight percent of the battle is with yourself. I can't stress this enough. If you can't convince yourself then you can't convince anybody else. You're the expert. You know what people need. Most people don't understand marketing.

They pretend they do but really they have no clue. They need you to tell them what to do. You need to be a force of confidence and you can't do that unless you have the right mindset. Now of course not everybody is 100% confident all the time.

What does confidence have to do with copywriting? Everything! If you're not confident in your copy then your client will know, the reader will know.

The first step in any sales process is knowing what your customer wants. How do you know you have the right target market? If you're selling to somebody in person than you need to ask three questions to make sure that you know what they want and if they can afford it. For example, a car salesperson will ask 'what you want to use the car for?' Perhaps she's talking to family and therefore needs a SUV to go to soccer games or hockey practice. If he's talking to you a single guy and his needs will be very different. You might want a fast sports car that will impress his girlfriend.

When you write a sales letter you don't necessarily have the luxury of asking those questions, unless you've done your research first. You'll need to use paid advertisements and detailed analytics of who your customer is to know how to target them correctly.

When somebody blends on your sales letter or opens your email they should be all already qualified. That means they should already have the budget and need of what you're selling.

Readers Read Ads as Individuals, Usually While They Are by Themselves

Don't address them as though they were a crowd in a stadium. It makes you seem cold and distant, when your aim is to be seen as a trusted friend. It also loses the reader's attention.

As you write your copy, think about the one person you are "talking" to. Pretend you are in a one-on-one conversation with that single reader, presenting information on what you are offering, "one human being to another, and second person *singular.*"

You can't bore people into doing what you want them to do. You can only *interest* them into doing it. Hold their interest by writing short sentences arranged in brief paragraphs. Don't use difficult words.

If you're not sure whether a word is too difficult for the average person, Ogilvy suggested you take a bus trip to Iowa, talk to a farmer for a week, then come back by train and talk to your fellow passengers. And then, at the end of that time, see if you still want to use that word.

There may be something dated in the way Ogilvy described this fact-finding adventure, but the advice is still valuable today. Listen to the people you want to appeal to, and then address them in language they understand and can relate to.

On Don't Write Essays

That means don't wax philosophic or get too theoretical. Your copy should tell your readers exactly what your product or service will do for them and how it will improve their lives. It should be conversational and easy to read.

Make sure your copy is filled with specifics that make it easy for readers to picture how they will personally benefit from using what you are offering them. You can paint them a picture instead of writing them an essay.

It is always a great advantage to be able to write copy in the form of a story. Telling a story is a great way to get and hold your prospects' attention. David Ogilvy gave us the hugely popular ad for Zippo lighters that used the headline:

"The amazing story of a Zippo that worked after being taken from the belly of a fish."

Not only do stories like these grab your prospects' interest, but people also remember stories, which can carry the influence of the ad (or the website copy or the blog) beyond the initial reading. Just make sure there's a strong connection between the story and the product so that remembering the story automatically brings up the image of the product.

Avoid using analogies. People often misunderstand analogies, especially if you don't have their undivided attention. For example, if you show a picture of a Rembrandt and say, "Just as a Rembrandt portrait is a masterpiece, so too is our product," many readers will think you're selling Rembrandt prints.

If they're not interested in buying a Rembrandt, they may not even read the rest of the piece. And superlatives ("We're simply the best in the world!") convince nobody.

Keep it simple stupid. This wasn't written by a copywriter but it might as well have been for it should be the copywriting mantra. You want to keep all your is simple and straightforward as possible. Don't try to be clever or use any jargon. The most famous lines ever written in the English language are to be or not to be by William Shakespeare. The six words out only one syllable long and not over three letters. Yet everybody instantly recognizes it from Hamlet. And not a single word is over three letters long. The lesson? Keep it simple stupid.

Good copy is ridding clear concise using simple words that can trek to the point. It's conversational and informal. It's clear and concise with simple words that get your point across. You can use fracture the occasional rule of grammar, if it helps to make your writing more digestible. Sentence fragments, one-sentence paragraphs, beginning with conjunctions and ending in prepositions are all fine, even desirable. And don't forget to use plenty of bullets and numbered lists. Think your audience is too sophisticated for this? Don't be so sure.

A recent study shows that more than 50 percent of students at school and more than 75 percent at two-year colleges in the United States could not: Interpret a table about exercise and blood pressure; Understand the arguments of newspaper editorials; or Compare credit card offers with different interest rates and annual fees. The bad news is that these kids are more literate than the average US adult, which is not that surprising considering that the vast majority of US adults have less education.

On Landing Pages

Successful marketers know that it's crazy to create a product or and then spoil the campaign by injecting the traffic straight through a nondescript home page. Any home page to a website is just a mess of choices and instructions won't get you any sales. Through a highly focused landing page with only one action available that can dramatically increase your sales and conversions and memberships want to sign up for an e-book download or product. But what makes a landing page so powerful? The secret is the ability to segment your audience so the reader feels like you are speaking strictly to them about their pain and how you can fix it. Using a highly targeted landing page you can grow your email subscriber's list faster sell more products in less time. But what is a landing page or a sales letter?

Landing pages are the modern equivalent to old fashion sales letters which used to be mail directly to prospects. A sales letter is an old term originally referred to a letter by post which was sent directly to the consumer so they would either phone in four mailed back a check. A sales letter as synonymous with sales page or sales copy.

Sales letters are still extremely effective but generally aren't as targeted and can be more expensive. But I'm a big believer in taking a look at what everybody else in the market is doing and doing the exact opposite. It's increasingly hard to stand out but one easy way is to take some old fashion techniques and make them relevant again. Kind of like bellbottom pants.

A copywriters' ability to create a great landing page or sales letter is critical. As you know, copy is designed to convince the reader to take some sort of action. This can be subscribing to email list or it can be to buy something directly.

Sales letters used to be sent through the mail but now with the revolutionary tool called the Internet and his easier to write a sales letter than ever before. Millions of people spend billions of dollars every day on the Internet. You can work from home and reach millions of people from Asia to Africa to South America. But now since so many people are doing it the competition has become even more fierce or. You have to get everything absolutely.

We will go through in detail the mechanics of a well laid out sales letter.

On Headlines

We've already spent a whole chapter talking about headlines so we won't go into much detail here but I want to reiterate the importance of a headline because it is IMPORTANT! (Hopefully you get it.) According to David Ogilvy, on average, five times as many people read the headlines as read the body copy. It follows that unless your headline sells your product, you have wasted most, if not all of your money.

I've written a lot about headlines so we won't go into more detail about here. In today's ADHD world where we scroll at a furious rate, swipe left and right, click, you have blessed the second two catch your reader's attention.

On The Pre-Header

You don't necessarily need a pre-header but it can be useful in attracting your target market. For example, you probably read something like: "Attention copywriters." Now if your copywriter you know that this sales letter is for you that most likely this sales letter will make you a better copywriter. You're targeting your prime prospect for your message and you are qualifying him or her.

On Leads

This is the first sentence of your sales letter and just like the headline is extremely important to capture the reader's attention. You shouldn't use what you've learned about headlines to write your lead. Eugene supports said that was the job of the headline and the lead to get the reader to go to the next sentence in the next sentence. The job of the headline and lead was not to sell but merely to peak interest.

Examples of a good lead are:

If you'd like to learn how to become a best-selling author but just didn't know where to start, then this information is for you.

This speaks to the reader's interest. Again it tells the reader who this sales letter is for. If you don't want to be an author and then read on.

On Body copy

This is the bulk of your text where you now have the reader's attention. In the body copy, you want to be very strategic about how you present your product. Don't let anybody persuade you that your body should be short. Of course, not everybody will read all your text, but it should be available for the undecided reader if he or she wants.

In the body copy you will have to establish rapport and build relationship with your reader. Remember that sales are built on trust. To build trus,t you have put yourself into your reader's shoes. You have to demonstrate you understand their pain and, in what they are going through.

I highly recommend that you put bullet points in your copy to summarize what you've already said. They:

- Are easy to read

- Break up the text into small chunks

- Make it easy to skim read

Most great copy have sort of bullet points in them.

Although not mandatory, you might consider telling a story sales letter just like the Wall Street Journal it. A great story to tell (and one you see everywhere) is called the 'Pain-to-Gain' story. This is a story about somebody who had a problem and then overcame some sort of challenge and now is successful and happy.

Perhaps one of the most famous (although perhaps not in a good way) Pain-to-Gain stories is probably Jared from the Subway commercials. The commercial showed the 'before' and 'after' picture of Jared and explain how he only ate Subway sandwiches to lose weight.

No matter your personal opinion about Jared, this is one of the most successful campaigns of all time and propelled Subway into the big leagues, right up there next to McDonalds.

It's best if the 'Pain-to-Gain' story is a personal story about how you or your customer went from broke to riches using XYZ strategy. Using a personal story gives you a couple of advantages. First of all, it makes you likable because it tells the reader that you aren't always this way but you managed to come out of ahead because of this proven strategy. Secondly, it shows the reader that you have authority and that you know what you're talking about. A lot of people are worried about telling personal stories because they think that they will lose credibility when in fact it is just the opposite. As long as you can show the reader how you've changed them you don't need to worry about them losing faith in your ability to deliver on the product.

You should also use testimonials in your body copy which, again, can paint a story or they can show how you took care of that customer. Testimonials are super powerful because it is a third-party verification that your solution works of all seen testimonials in many forms and we know that they work.

People are smart and most people have a sixth sense when it comes to fake testimonials. You have to have real people talking and not just actors to make the testimonial as believable and authentic as possible. These days it is easy to get a video testimonial with your camera phones. All you need to do is get them to talk to the camera. It doesn't need to be anything elaborate or have a high production value. If you want, you can give them a script with the format you want your testimonial in but it's not necessary.

Creating the ultimate landing page is not as hard as you think but there are some simple rules that you need to follow in order to get high conversion.

You have only about two seconds to capture your prospects' attention when you do that through an incredible headline. Landing pages live or die by the headline. Often a better headline alone will boost the effectiveness of your landing page and even overcome some of the other mistakes you can make.

Having a complicated landing page is by far one of the biggest mistakes, made especially by young copywriters or inexperienced companies. You only want your landing page to do one thing and thing only. Do not have two opt-ins for two different target markets. This confuses the reader and will lower your conversion rate. The paradox of choice reveals that when given multiple options the decision ends up being not being able to choose at all. An effective landing pages ask for one specific action and that's it not asking for the sale. Sales pages are direct and to the point. You need to ask for the sale. This is not a blog where you do some soft selling. People have come here because they want to buy and it's your job to make sure that they do that.

A common rookie mistake is to use pay-per-click and send all the traffic to the website where it usually goes to die. I'm sorry to say I'm sorry to say I've made this mistake many times. Most websites are not designed or optimized for conversions. That's like being dumped off at the front door of a stranger's house and told to find the bathroom. The visitor might search around some and then opt to pee in the bushes.

If people aren't told what to do, they'll get lost and wander to that Instagram post with the cute kittens. Unless you are determined you do what most other people do when it comes to your website is the turnaround and bounce rate. You need to test your landing pages like you would test everything else.

Most websites use fancy WordPress themes that aren't designed to convert sales. These websites are used more for visual presentation which is fine for branding and for company information but aren't going to get users to buy your product or service. Cut out the clutter and create the cleanest and simplest page possible if you want some action.

If you're landing page is using ugly graphics, fonts, colours, clipart, and not be visually appealing then you will lose credibility. That's not to say that you can't have a simple landing page, but it should look professional. Use fonts and styles that would be typically used in that industry. For example, you cannot use a post-modern design look for an oil and gas company. People expect a little bit of animation and moving graphics these days. If you're like most copywriters you're not very graphically inclined but likely there are plenty of programs out there that can easily create landing pages for you or you can hire a graphic artist or web developer to do for you.

Did you know that most readers spend 80% of their time above the fold? (aka before they start scrolling). That means you have to pay extra attention to the first third of your landing page (and website).

Spend most of your time working on the headline, the first paragraph and your offer. Everything after that is just gravy.

Don't be lazy or shy about grabbing and holding your reader's attention. It's simply and sleep gets the benefit of your product or offer the way you do. Don't overestimate your credibility. Readers a far more skeptical than ever before. Think about your landing page from your prospect and ask other people to look at it see if they feel compelled to take the action you're looking for.

You need a clear 'Call to Action' whether it's a graphic button or hyperlinked text to both tell your visitor what they need to do. You need a minimum of two calls to action but preferably four or five even depending on how long the landing page is. One of the first fold so those who know right away they want to buy can just click and go on the way. Those who are little more skeptical can read below the fold and click on the buy button at the very bottom

Be crystal clear is about your goals and keep in mind your body copy on point as a logical progression from the headline on offer. Anytime you digress is a conversion lost. Most visitors are scammers and skipping through your copy at least in the beginning. Remember people always skim first before they decide if it's worth reading. But even then people read the beginnings and ends before they read the middles. Make sure you keep your most critical and persuasive arguments in those positions.

Make your first paragraph short, no more than one or two lines. Vary your paragraph length here. It helps create visual appeal and makes it easier to read your copy. No paragraph should be more than 45 lines long a time. Consider how much of your content should be seen above the fold on the first screen. You should have the header and maybe a subheadline but no more than that. Your visitors can still scroll downward to read your testimonials your bullet points and other components so no matter where your visitor is an act NOW link or button remains visible. Remove all extraneous matter from your landing page. This includes navigation bars visual clutter's social media links and links to websites. You want the reader focused solely on your copy is supportive visual elements offer you not want them to wander around lost.

Don't ask for information you don't need us you absolutely need a phone number for whatever reason don't ask for don't ask for date of birth income or any extraneous information. This has constantly proven to lower conversion rates.

The most important part of marketing as with landing pages is to assume nothing and test everything. It's because something worked in the past does not mean you work in the future and something that didn't work as a means it's can continue to be dead in the future.

Unlike most direct mail, however, the web is a strongly visual medium. Good design helps support the content, leading the visitor's eye from here to there and directing them through your message layer by layer, step by step. This is especially so in the formatting of an effective landing page.

That's why I'll devote myself to the overall look, feel, and formatting of effective landing pages for this article. Copywriters don't have to be designers. But copywriters who understand effective landing design fundamentals — what works and what doesn't — will be better able to work and share ideas with designers. That means you and your entire creative team will be on board and working toward the common goal of capturing more conversions.

Go through their conversion process and note the places where you feel a bit stumped or put off. Then go back to your own landing page and compare. Consider what you could revise or eliminate for better effect. Put your most critical landing page elements in the upper 300 pixels of the page.

Usability research shows over half of your site visitors won't scroll "below the fold," so forget the warm-up copy, get right to the point, and keep your value proposition at first screen view. Think simple: Use a one-column format with ample margins and white space to increase reading comprehension. Break up big paragraphs into smaller paragraphs – and no more than 5 lines per paragraph. You want to encourage visitors to read and engage with your message. Your readers will always scan your copy first before they decide it's worth their while to read it. Dense-looking copy doesn't get read. Period. Be obvious and use standard usage conventions: Underline your links, be clear, descriptive, and specific when describing them. No visitor should have to work to use your page or understand your message.

Make sure your page loads quickly. Depending on your marketing and your product or service mix, strive for a 3-second or less page load. This is also good from an SEO standpoint. This may seem obvious but it's not something that copywriters think a lot about. Don't plump your page with unnecessary graphics or videos. Optimize essential graphics to reduce file size and load time.

If you are using Wordpress then there all sorts of plugins you can use to optimize your site and compress your code and cache your site. If you're using something like Wix, Squarespace or Weebly, there is little you can do other than pay for faster hosting.

Use the same color palette from your ads on your landing page. There should be a smooth, consistent flow to help keep your prospect oriented and assured that they are indeed "landed" in the right place. Choose a single dominant photo image to be your hero shot: Use a product photo or, in the case of a service, you could use your logo or even a photo of your location. Make it clickable and don't forget to add a benefit-rich caption.

Put your message, copy, or image close to the middle of your page. Less critical elements can be placed in sidebars or perhaps even eliminated. Make it easy to complete your input form: For example, have the input cursor hop instantly from field to field upon completion. Let your user tab around fields. No drop-down menus require only a checkbox action. And my personal favorite — auto-populate any fields you can.

Remember, your landing page is your visitor's last stop to buy something outright or Step 2 if lead generation is your goal. Whether it's one step or one of many, your copy and design has to focus on firing up your visitor's self-interest as well as build their confidence and trust in your product/service and in you and your company. Therefore, be honest, forthright, and leave the "cheese" behind.

Focus on one objective for each page. Define your objective and drive everything on the page to it. Sales pages should use a vertical flow through the center of the page. For pages that offer a single benefit (service or product), vertical single-column body copy through the center of the page consistently performs better than other layouts and should always be tested. Left or right columns should be used to support shifting eye movement toward the page objective. For example, a good example is if you want your visitor to read your testimonials.

One of the changes they made, for example, was to swap out the left-column navigation, replace it with testimonials, and move the navigation to the far-right column. You could try that, or move the navigation to the bottom of the page, or delete it.

Eliminate elements that may distract the sight path from flow toward the objective. If page elements such as photos and graphic images don't move your visitor briskly to taking the desired action, dump them. Every element on the page has to work in concert toward the same goal. Use visual elements to draw attention toward the call to action. Don't guess. Test it all to find what works best for you.

Avoid using off-page links and if you do, make sure they pop up in a separate window. Use passive pop-ups or launch new browser windows when needed to provide details or supplemental decision information. Once visitors have left the page, their forward momentum is interrupted and must be re-established even if they do return. By eliminating the number of clicks it takes to act, you keep a visitor longer and more engaged with your message. No surprises here for me.

Define your objective and stick with it. Make sure every word, graphic, icon keeps your prospect focused on the one single action that will satisfy the single, most important objective.

Not as easy as I make it sound, I know. Clients tend to want to "kitchen sink" every pixel of web page real estate. They want to maximize profits and they think the best way to do that is to add an offer to every piece of real estate. Make sure you keep your evidence and test results like these close at hand.

How is an Effective Landing Page Like a Direct Mail Letter?

They're both formatted for one column. Long and short, the one-column format converts best every time. This explains the stubborn effectiveness of everyone's favorite online long-form sales letters. Garish? Sometimes. Too long? Perhaps. But they work, in part, because there are no other distractions for the reader. Even with all the insets, widgets and gadgets, each is firmly ensconced within the one column. Further, the one-column format lets readers know that there's more to look for below the fold of the first screen. The convention of the letter like, one-column design tells them so.

Like the traditional sales letter, the one-column landing page offers a step-by-step selling sequence for your reader. The headline moves the reader to the subhead, etc. Add columns filled with links, even something as simple as navigational links, and you've given the reader a reason to look and click away from your message. Nick says, and I concur, one-column may be the best way to go. Test it yourself and see if it makes a difference.

In fact, it's still the best online method for converting prospects into customers or clients. A critical part of the process begins, however, before a single email is sent. You've got to get people on your list in the first place. This happens most effectively at a landing page specifically designed to convince the right people to sign up. Some people call these opt-in landing pages "squeeze" pages, which, in addition to being a derogatory way to think about the process, is also technically incorrect.

On The Squeeze Page

Here's a quick Internet marketing history lesson: a squeeze page was originally a very specific type of opt-in page which required you to supply an email address just for the privilege of reading a sales letter. If you didn't buy immediately, you got follow-up pitches. Things were easier back then until marketers realized the potential of the internet and everybody jumped aboard. Now the internet is so crowded and there is so much competition everything needs to be a well-oiled machine to succeed.

I'm about to show you how to win the trust and interest of prospective subscribers despite any initial misgivings your audience may have. Here are some things to think about.

The first step is crucial, and yet time and again I see people plow ahead without a clear understanding of exactly the type of person they want on their email list. Without a clear and detailed understanding of who you want, you can't craft a message that resonates strongly enough to spark interest and gain trust. The exact same course benefits could attract your typical "get rich quick" business opportunity type. But instead, the message is positioned squarely against that type of person, and aimed at people who are willing to put the effort in.

Take the time to figure out who you really want on your list. What is your ultimate goal? What is going to moving enough people from suspects to prospects and ultimately to customer or client? Then - and only then - will you know how to "speak their language" with your opt-in copy.

Your email opt-in page has one goal — to get people to sign up to your email list. Every word and element of the page should support that single action. If it doesn't, lose it. That means lose your typical sidebar. That means lose those links in your copy. In many cases, that means creating a page so focused on the opt-in that you take an approach that's different from your normal site design. One page, one action. That's it.

What are the essential elements? No exceptions, you absolutely must have: The headline: You've got to instantly catch attention with your headline. The benefits: You've got to tell by teasing, usually with fascinating bullet points. The call to action: You've got to expressly tell people to sign-up. The opt-in form: You've got to have a way for them to sign-up.

You should also have some kind of social proof. The number of subscribers, subscriber testimonials, reviews, and media mentions, etc. Whether or not you need to add in proof depends on a number of criteria, including the strength of your brand and the traffic source.

For example, if you're driving existing blog subscribers to a focused email list, your good reputation precedes you. If you're using Google AdWords to drive traffic, you likely have no reputation on your side and you'll need everything you've got.

What incentive should you give? It's always been a smart tactic to offer an up-front incentive, or "ethical bribe" to convince people to sign up for your list. This could be a free report, webinar, audio seminar, or other instant gratification freebie. In many markets, this strategy still works just fine. In others, you'll face savvy subscribers who snag your incentive with a "junk mail" email address, or simply unsubscribe immediately. The better approach is to focus the incentive on staying subscribed. Offer that report over time as a series of emails from your autoresponder, break the video or audio into parts, and always entice subscribers with what's coming next. The key is for people to realize that you're giving more than you're taking, and they'll happily stay with you much longer.

The less form data you ask for, the more people sign up. Almost all the opt-in tests show that if just ask for email rather than name and email you get a much higher response. If your business goals dictate getting more information, like a mailing address and phone number, so be it. Where I live, in Vancouver, the real estate market is so hot people don't mind giving more information, like a phone number, for a landing page advertising a presale condo. They know if they don't act fast, they will miss out on a valuable piece of property. And of course, a phone number is a valuable piece of personal information, especially for a realtor.

However, in most cases, people don't want to give a phone number. I'd get the prospect on the list first, and then send valuable content that culminates with a call to action that asks for that information via a contact form. The more trust you build, the more people open up to you. And you get to communicate with prospects regularly, which means it's no longer an all-or nothing situation.

Everything above represents tried-and-tested wisdom for email opt-in pages. But when it comes down to what specifically works for you and your audience, only your own split-testing will tell the whole truth. Changes to headlines, button colors, and other tiny tweaks can make a big difference when it comes to your opt-in rate. Just don't forget step one above.

In other words, tweaking your landing page to get the absolute best opt-in rate doesn't mean much if you're attracting the wrong people for your ultimate goal of selling something. You need to make sure you test within the bounds of a well-targeted premise that resonates with your intended audience.

They discovered that email campaigns that opened with promise and decent click through ratios generally died on the vine with ill-conceived, poorly designed or just plain lazy landing pages. Bored, confused prospects quickly took their conversion clicks — and wallets — elsewhere. Even the "big boys" with the deep pockets still fail to think about their email/landing page campaign as a whole project. What happens is that all the care and craft is lavished on the email part, while the landing page — if used at all — gets "ugly sister" attention.

We've spent a lot of time exploring the copy and design techniques that drive successful landing pages. But do you know how to best measure your success?

Let's consider some of the benchmark numbers. What exactly is a conversation rate? It's the percentage of visitors that turn into a lead, sale, or some other desired outcome. Every business and industry is different. I work with a lot of authors and it's not unusual to see conversion rates of 40%. Why? Because the target market are ultra fans and books are entertaining. If you're selling entertainment them.

A retail site is frequently considered a success when its conversion is in the high single digits, but for lead generation sites, numbers in the high teens are considered good. An average retail site is converting about 1 to 2 percent of visitors and an average lead generation site is doing 5 to 6 percent. Do the math. That's a whopping number of folks not responding, not clicking, and not buying. How can you calculate a purchase conversion rate? It's simple. Using your site's analytics package (see recommendations below), locate the number of unique visitors during a given period and divide that by the number of sales transactions during the same period. If you are 2 percent or less, the good news is that you have plenty of room to grow your business. Increase your transactions by even one.

On Subheadings

If your text is more than a couple paragraphs long, you need subheadlines that separate the text from each other. (Just like in this book.) These are important to break up the main body copy. You should put almost as much thought into these as you do your main headline. Most readers will scan sales letter begin with to see if it's something worth their time. They are read the subheadlines to see if they're interesting and only then will they go back to the start at the very beginning.

On The Structure of Persuasive Copy

Writing great copy takes work and a little flair. Some of it is how it feels when you read it but there is also a little science. If you follow the guidelines below you'll be well on your way to becoming an A-list copywriter.

Let's dig into the nuts and bolts of what makes great persuasive copy. We've seen that the purpose of each element of copy is designed to get the first sentence read, then from there keep the reader engaged step by step to the conclusion. We know to keep things clear, concise and simple so that our writing communicates with ease. And we definitely understand the make-or-break importance of an attention-grabbing headline.

So how do we then structure our content to be persuasive? Good content structure is never written in stone, but persuasive copy will do certain things and contain certain elements time and time again. Whether you're writing a sales page, an email, a long blog post, or promotional ebook, the flow will determine effectiveness. First of all, focus on the reader – make an important promise early on with your headline and opening paragraphs that tells the reader what's in it for her. Never allow readers to question why they are bothering to pay attention. Each separate part of your narrative should have a main idea –something compelling and a main purpose which supports your bigger point and promise. Don't digress, and don't ramble. Stay laser focused.

Be ultra-specific in your assertions, and always make sure to give "reasons why." General statements which are unsupported by specific facts cause a reader to go on high alert. Demonstrate large amounts of credibility, using statistics, expert references, and testimonials as appropriate. You must be authoritative – if you're not an existing expert on a subject, you'd better have done your research. After building your credibility and authority, make sure you get back to the most important person — the reader. What's still in it for him? Restate the hook and the promise that got readers engaged in the first place. Make an offer. Whether you're selling a product or selling an idea, you've got to explicitly present it for acceptance by the reader. Be bold and firm when you present your offer, and relieve the reader's risk of acceptance by standing behind what you say. Sum everything up, returning full circle to your original promise and demonstrate how you've fulfilled it.

These are some of the key elements of persuasive copy. As always there are no hard and fast rules with copy, but if use theses as points as a roadmap to your writing, you'll achieve better results. Now that you know the basics of creating persuasive copy, let's dig into one particular element of copywriting that often trips up beginners — features and benefits.

Sell with benefits and support with features. This is important! One of the most repeated rules of compelling marketing is to stress benefits, not features. In other words, identify the underlying benefit that each feature of a product or service provides to the prospect, because that's what will prompt the purchase. This is one rule that always applies, except when it doesn't. We'll look at the exceptions in a bit. Fake Benefits The idea of highlighting benefits over features seems simple. But it's often tough to do in practice. Writers often end up with fake benefits instead.

Have you heard of the "forehead slap" test? Use it to see if your copy truly contains a benefit to the reader. In other words, have you ever woken up from a deep sleep, slapped yourself in the forehead, and exclaimed "I need more iron!" It doesn't happen. Getting someone to pull out their wallet to buy that so-called "benefit" will be difficult at best.

The real benefit hidden in that headline. Nobody really wants more iron. But anyone in his or her right mind does want to avoid the side effects such as low energy levels, headaches, and shortness of breath. A person with low iron will want to avoid the negative effects. That is the true benefit that the example product offers.

How do you successfully extract true benefits from features? Here's a four-step process that works: First, make a list of every feature of your product or service. Second, ask yourself why each feature is included in the first place. Third, take the "why" and ask "how" does this connect with the prospect's desires? Fourth, get to the absolute root of what's in it for the prospect at an emotional level.

What's in it for them? Getting to the emotional root is crucial for effective consumer sales. But what about business prospects? When Features Work When selling to business or highly technical people, features alone can sometimes do the trick. Pandering to emotions will only annoy them. Besides, unlike consumers who mostly "want" things rather than "need" them, business and tech buyers often truly need a solution to a problem or a tool to complete a task.

When a feature is well known and expected from your audience, you don't need to sell it. However, with innovative features, you still need to move the prospect down the four-step path. While the phrase "contains an artificial intelligence algorithm" may be enough to get the Slashdot reader salivating, he'll still want to know how it works and what it does for him. The 'what's in it for me?' aspect remains crucial.

For business buyers, you're stressing "bottom line" benefits from innovative features. If you can demonstrate that the prospect will be a hero because your CRM product will save her company $120,000 a year compared to the current customer relationship management choice, you've got a good shot. While that may seem like a no-brainer purchase to you, you'll still need to strongly support the promised benefit with a detailed explanation of how the features actually deliver. Change scares the business buyer, because it's their job or small business on the line if the product disappoints. Remember sell with benefits and support with features!

You need to know how to craft a truly compelling offer. Let's look at some guidelines for creating offers in our next section. "Kids Eat Free" and other irresistible offers. The sign says it all — "Kids Eat Free Every Monday and Tuesday." That's called an offer. It's not the restaurant's main offering which is trading food for money.

They've made an appealing offer that cause people to take action. "Offer" is a contractual term. It's an invitation to enter into an economic relationship, or any relationship really. The relationship is based on mutual promises. I'll do this for you if you give me money or attention or sex or friendship. If there's no acceptance of the invitation, there's no contract and no relationship

You must then live the story and fulfill the offer. It's helpful to think about offers as coming in two varieties – primary and promotional. I'll highlight a couple of Joyner's favorite irresistible offers to demonstrate one of each type. Primary Offers: Federal Express originated with an idea expressed in a Yale undergraduate term paper authored by founder Fred Smith, which according to popular lore received a C from his skeptical professor. The company filled a huge need at the time, because the monopolistic United States Postal Service provided unacceptable results to important people, mainly on Wall Street.

Fred took Wall Street's money and became essential by providing an offer that couldn't be refused – guaranteed overnight delivery. That's it. A simple – yet powerful – idea. About the only thing this offer doesn't communicate is price. If the price wasn't right, FedEx would not have blasted off; but in the early days, price wasn't the first question Wall Street brokers asked about if it really, absolutely, positively had to be there the next morning. Wall Street would much rather pay a premium price for important documents since every day their documents were delayed could mean a loss of thousands of dollars.

Let's look at another guarantee. Domino's Pizza Tom Monaghan entered the world of pizza with a single location he bought in 1960. Pizza is a tough business – it's the only food item that has its own category in the Yellow Pages, and there are always several shops to choose from in any reasonably populated area. While trying to expand the business, Monaghan faced near bankruptcy and franchise disputes that almost buried Domino's. But one single promotional idea changed everything and put Domino's in an overwhelmingly dominant position in this ultra-competitive field: 30 minutes or less or it's free. That simple guarantee was explosive. The secret to the offer's success resides in the nature of your average tired, hungry, time-strapped citizen. What seems like the safer bet – the tastiest pizza in town with unpredictable timing, or the pizza that arrives in a half an hour or else ends up a free meal? The irony is, back before Domino's had to discontinue the offer in 1993 due to an auto injury lawsuit, the pizza sucked. Some think it still does. Each day, millions of people in more than 60 countries eat Domino's.

Make an Offer It's troubling to see so many entities trying to gain business online, yet without ever making a compelling offer. There's no apparent reason why someone should select you from the overcrowded field, because often you've made no express offer at all. So many websites assume that a visitor will get the obvious value that the owner knows he provides. Value is communicated through offers, however, and those offers must be communicated quickly and explicitly.

Consider your own surfing habits for a second, and ask yourself – why would my target audience be any different? In the lingo of direct-response copywriting, an offer is a call to action. For bloggers, desired actions include having a reader subscribe, bookmark you, make comments, respond to surveys, share your post on social networking sites, and utilize your information resources that double as sales tools. Start making offers if you want some action.

For example, my guarantee for this book would be this book is the best book on copywriting. I Guarantee It! There you have it. You just can't go wrong reading this book. We've guaranteed your satisfaction. Those are powerful words, right? But what does our guarantee really mean? What if you think this book is marginal at best? I'm not offering you refund your money and I can't give you back your valuable time if you feel it was wasted. There is no power without proof. In advertisements proclaiming "satisfaction guaranteed" are fairly common – and that's the problem: the statement can come across as just another hollow promise because it often is. Every promise you make to a prospect should be both fulfilled and guaranteed. When you sell something in exchange for someone's hard-earned money, the promise is that the product or service will meet, or exceed, expectations. The guarantee means you will give the money back if the buyer feels that's not actually the case.

The word guarantee is extremely powerful, but only coupled with evidence of substance. The proof behind the guarantee accomplishes two things – it demonstrates confidence in your offering and relieves the risk to the buyer. Confidence and Risk Every contemplated purchase carries risk to the buyer. Before consumer protection laws, the rule was caveat emptor (let the buyer beware), and these days buyers are still cautious, even leery – especially of unknown vendors.

Even when already emotionally and logically committed to what you have to offer, buyers don't want to make a mistake. It's up to you to help them get over the hump. The way to get past the buyer's uncertainty is to first demonstrate confidence in your offering. Not through boasts or sales prattle, but with a good old-fashioned, no-questions-asked, "money-where-my-mouth-is" cash-back guarantee. Return periods of 30, 60 or 90 days work great. Some direct marketers go as far as 6 months, a year, or even a lifetime, money-back guarantee. The longer the better.

Other techniques involve a "return premium." The seller allows you to keep all or part of the materials delivered even after the refund or promises to pay you double your money back (or some other multiple). Now that's confidence, and it speaks directly to the buyer's lingering reservations.

You've now created a risk-free buying environment. Your conversion of prospects to customers will skyrocket compared to the same offer, sans guarantee. Guaranteed Higher Profits "Whoa there," many of you are saying, "I can't do that kind of thing. It's way too risky for me." Our first response might be to ask you how much faith you have in your offering. If your faith is lacking, improve your product or service. As we've seen with Domino's Pizza and Federal Express the guarantee was the key that made the offers irresistible. But you've spotted the essence of the technique – you're taking the buyer's risk and shifting it over to yourself.

Assuming the faith in your offering is there, here's why you shouldn't be concerned: First of all, you will get some returns, no matter how much value you deliver. The reason is that your guarantee will generate a much higher number of sales. By taking the risk away from the buyer, invariably you'll sell to someone who the product wasn't suited for. That's okay; the numbers are working for you.

Your returns will be lower than you think, even among those who experience buyer's remorse. We like to remain consistent on a psychological basis, and our brains work hard to validate our earlier decisions. Couple that with the ambivalence people experience when faced with initiating the return process (especially for physical products), and the sale remains in place.

When it comes to information products, some people will rip you off. They'll happily consume the knowledge you offer, and still demand a refund. If your product is digital, some will share your hard work with other people, and you won't make a dime. Don't worry about it. Believe it or not, most people are honest. Don't lose sleep over those that are not. Your sales (and profits) are up, perhaps dramatically, because of your guarantee. That was the goal, right? There are certainly other methods to keep customers happy and minimize returns, but the general rule is to always make a strong, substantive guarantee that actually transfers the reader's risk back over to you. Now that you're comfortable with the basics of offers, guarantees, and writing about features vs. benefits, let's take a look at some unique ways to write persuasive copy.

While great writing is truly an art, those looking to improve their craft as a copywriter can find a lot of help from behavioral psychology and neuroscience studies. The only problem is that good writers are often busy people, and they don't have time to slog through dry research papers to find an interesting nugget or two.

You're watching football, and your team's quarterback gets slammed with a bone-crunching tackle, snapping a rib. Can't you just feel yourself cringing at the thought? That's the power of mirror neurons and how they affect the human mind.

According to research on the subject, these neurons activate when you observe something happening, and then transfer some of the feelings, if it's powerful enough, on to you. It's likely that they're biologically useful for necessary evolutionary traits, such as empathy, or "walking in someone else's shoes." Although a majority of the current research on mirror neurons focuses on literal observation, great writers know that strong emotions can be conveyed through words as well.

Think about the first example … if you did cringe at the thought of a man breaking his ribs, you're already experiencing this effect in action!

When crafting compelling copy, you have to understand what keeps your potential reader up at night. It's easy for us to write out, "Envision this …," but it's not as easy to get people to care. You have to speak to a feeling that's already there – not try to force one on your reader.

If you're selling software that takes the hassle out of content optimization, you need to speak to the frustrated entrepreneur who's tired of nitpicking and game-playing for Google, and who wants to get back to writing.

If you're selling beer, you need to invoke memories of good times spent with friends over an ice-cold beverage. Using this information on mirror neurons to transfer a desired feeling onto readers is effective, but it's only going to work if you know what makes those readers tick.

Be wary of "selling" savings Here's something you should know — if you're using precious real estate to chest thump about your low prices, you're doing it wrong. Not only has research shown us that asking customers to directly compare prices is a bad idea, but a study from Stanford University has revealed that that selling "time" is far more effective (for most businesses) than selling money.

Jennifer Aaker, the lead researcher in the Stanford study, sought to explain why companies like Miller would use a slogan such as "It's Miller Time!"

As an inexpensive beer, shouldn't they be promoting their reasonable prices instead? It turns out, no. A person's experience with a product tends to foster feelings of personal connection with it, referring to time typically leads to more favorable attitudes — and to more purchases. What does this have to do with writing great copy?

Writing compelling copy helps you speak to what really matters to your buyer — and that's their time, troubles, and objectives. We know that customers are willing to pay more for exceptional service, but you also need to understand that they're willing to pay your prices if you speak to them in a way that shows you value what they hope to achieve. Your efforts will be perceived as far more genuine and effective than trying to sell them on bottom-dollar prices.

Time is a scarce resource — once it's gone, it's gone — and therefore it's more meaningful to us. Sweat the small stuff This is an incredibly important study for copywriters and conversion experts. A fascinating piece of research from Carnegie Mellon University was able to show that the devil really is in the details, especially when it comes to creating copy that converts.

In the study, researchers tested how changing a single phrase would affect conversions over the long haul. They did this by setting up a free DVD trial program that customers could sign up for, and testing it between two different phrases:

"A \$5 fee" and "A small \$5 fee"

I bet you even feel the difference as you read the copy. You add just one word and guess what happens? They found that the second phrase was able to increase signup rates by over 20%. The science behind it is pretty interesting. Researchers found that this emphasis on the "small" fee made it far easier to deal with conservative spenders, also known as "tightwad" customers. Even though you are adding additional unnecessary words they have an emotional impact. We all know \$5 is a small fee to pay for anything these days. We don't really need the word "small" yet it obviously has an impact and helps persuade people that \$5 really *is* small.

When it comes to great copywriting, however, the lesson is more in the art of great writing rather than in the "science." You must take the time to measure, improve, and track the success of your craft. Great writers today have no excuses for not testing their work, so make sure you're sweating the small stuff and keeping tabs on how it performs.

A big mistake that many copywriters make is making little effort to be authentic. Everything is high-level: they promise the world, and since many consumers, especially in today's market, are hesitant to believe crazy claims, they're more likely to glaze over your copy, rather than get swept up by it. The answer? Create strong copy that addresses their objections head-on.

You might be familiar with the term "devil's advocate," which is when someone takes a position they don't inherently agree with in order to prove a point. This term comes from when the Catholic church used to use a person called the "devil's advocate" when they canonized someone into sainthood. Their job was to find flaws with the person so the debate around them was impartial. They ended the practise because you'll soon see that playing the devil's advocate actually enhances the persuasiveness of the original argument.

A study by social psychologist Charlan Nemeth was able to show that arguments framed in the "devil's advocate" style were more likely to persuade listeners to support the original argument, rather than to disagree with it. Nemeth has concluded that this occurs because potential flaws and concerns are brought up and subsequently addressed when engaging in the devil's advocate style, either by the speaker, or — subliminally — by the listener.

You're much more likely to be persuaded if the speaker says something like: Many of you are probably worried about whether I'm the right copywriter to hire right now because I'm too expensive or haven't worked in your industry but let me assure you my last five clients gave me amazing testimonials which you can see on my website.

Because your concerns are put in the spotlight, instead of being ignored or swept under the rug. So instead of trying to paint a picture of an infallible offer, point out common concerns that customers may have — then assure them with facts and evidence that they have nothing to worry about.

Don't rely on adjectives alone. Some writers might not agree with this, but college kids will tell you: an admissions letter is one of the most stressful pieces of persuasive copy you can write. And believe me, it is very much a piece of selling copy — you're selling you to some person who decides the fate of your future. Interestingly enough, in this analysis of persuasive admission letters — as discussed by the Harvard MBA admissions director who read them — verbs beat out adjectives more often than not.

Verbs get specific and are harder to ignore, especially in a vain world where everybody describes themselves with the same trite adjectives. How about this example. Verbs get in your face, and since your competitors will be fluffing up their copy with adjectives they found in a thesaurus, you can win people over by describing what you actually do. Include "power" words Smart copywriters know that there are certain persuasive words that hold more sway than others.

'You' is extremely powerful. According to recent research examining brain activation, few things light us up quite like seeing our own names in print or on the screen. Our names are intrinsically tied to our self-perception, and we become more engaged, and even more trusting of a message when our name appears in it.

According to certain MRI studies, few words light up our mid-brain quite like those that invoke a sense of fast reward. Let people know you'll solve their problems quickly, and they'll be more prone to buy.

'New' is another great word to use. Novelty plays an incredibly important role in activating our brain's reward center and in keeping us happy with our purchases. The research shows that perceived "newness" is important for a product, but can actually be damaging for a brand. People trust brands that have been around for a long time.

Do you have a better understanding of how to improve your persuasive copy using these techniques? Then let's address one of the biggest questions beginning copywriters ask. On handling objections

Because most people were subjected to thousands of ads a day, people are generally guarded when it comes to sales messages. You need to figure out what people are saying about your product. What reasons are people giving to not buying? And are they valid? Almost always some of these objections will be actual objections while some will just be limited buying beliefs.

You want to create a list of everything negative or perceived negative about the product on one piece of paper. You then want to address these had on.

Usually a copywriter will try to hide all the negative points about a product or service and hope that the reader doesn't find them. But that's almost always ends in folly. The audience is smart and they will figure out your being phony from a mile away. Once they do that they start to lose trust in you and your writing. If there are some negatives about your product, don't be shy about pointing them out.

The reader is going to figure it out anyways, so it's better to be straightforward and honest in the first place. Remember the biggest obstacle that salespeople need to overcome is the trust factor. Let's take, for example, you are selling a beauty product. It is prudent not to overpromise and say you look 20 years younger when it won't. There are some famous copywriters who used exaggerated headlines to great effect but in today's market they've been used so much they have lost their effect. Nobody falls for the "20 years younger" line anymore.

Even better then advertising a negative is to turn it into a positive. There are many famous campaigns that do this. Remember the Volkswagen campaign? Avis also did this in their famous slogan "we're second, we try harder." Take your list of negatives and examine them again. Are they really negative? How can they create an edge over your competition?

You're not as well-known as your competition? Bigger isn't always better. Do you remember the famous 1984 Apple ad? In the 80's, Apple was the little guy. They were up against the monolithic IBM which had a large grasp on the market share. The ad ran in the Super Bowl and is often voted as the best commercial of all time by all types of advertisement magazines.

In Steve Jobs' 1983 keynote Address he started off with this monologue:

```
It is now 1984.
```

```
It appears IBM wants it all. Apple is
perceived to be the only hope to offer IBM a
run for its money. Dealers initially
welcoming IBM with open arms now fear an IBM
dominated and controlled future. They are
increasingly turning back to Apple as the
only force that can ensure their future
freedom.
```

    IBM wants it all and is aiming its guns on its last obstacle to industry control: Apple.

    Will *Big Blue* dominate the entire computer industry? The entire information age? Was George Orwell right about 1984?"

By addressing the negatives about Apple, Jobs and his marketing team were able to paint Apple as David vs Goliath. But he makes the battle seem even more epic by the language used in the commercial. By using words like 'dominate', 'control', 'freedom' Apple is portrayed as the good guys against the evil IBM empire.

It's brilliant marketing. Today Apple is the big guys and IBM is nowhere to be found in the personal computer space. I sometimes wonder if a newer computer company could come along today and use the same psychology, portraying Apple as the evil conglomerate now that Apple is the dominant player in the electronics space.

Another potential negative may be that not everyone is suitable candidate for your product. Don't ignore this issue. Maybe it's too expensive for most people or maybe it's only available in limited quantities.

If you state that your product is not for everyone and there is limitations on who would get the benefit from it, then the reader will see that you are honest and not making outrageous claims. Maybe a product requires buyers to do something on order to get the benefit of what you're offering, something that they may not want to do, for example, go to the gym three times a week.

Tell them honestly what you can do and give them the right explanation. Ideal customers will be able to imagine from the outset how they will arrange the time to go to the gym. Most people will see that you are making a reasonable request and not promising to much.

To use Apple as an example again, they didn't portray themselves as the computer for everybody. If you were young, cool, hip and liked elegant design this was the computer for you. They were honest in the way they marketed themselves and their idea consumers lapped it up.

This can also prevent complications down the line as people will get angry that you made them buy something that wasn't right for them.

If you write good copy you can even use the power of exclusivity. By telling your reader that this product is not for everybody, it will actually make them want it more. The older generation who wanted to be young and hip again bought Apple computers and Apple Ipods and Apple phones.

Use a little reverse psychology on them. Remember as a kid when your mom said you couldn't watch that R-rated movie? You probably didn't care about the plots but the fact that it was R-rated made you want to watch it even more. If your mom let you watch those movies then all the sex and violence quickly lost its appeal.

Everyone has an opinion, but no one has a guarantee.

The Wall Street Journal ran one of the most famous and the most successful sales letters of all time. It was written by Martin Conroy and was used continuously for 28 years making it not only most successful but the longest-running and history.

By some accounts, it generated an astounding $2 billion worth of sales. However, Conroy's idea wasn't completely original. He took the idea from legendary copywriter Bruce Barton who wrote an ad for the Alexander Hamilton Institute in 1919.

This goes to show that the 'Big Idea never goes out of style. Most the thing if you create an amazing sales letter you can continue to use it. Great sales letters never go out of fashion.

Dear Reader:

On a beautiful late spring afternoon, twenty-five years ago, two young men graduated from the same college. They were very much alike, these two young men. Both had been better than average students, both were personable and both - as young college graduates are - were filled with ambitious dreams for the future.

Recently, these two men returned to college for their 25th reunion.

They were still very much alike. Both were happily married. Both had three children. And both, it turned out, had gone to work for the same Midwestern manufacturing company after graduation, and were still there.

But there was a difference. One of the men was manager of a small department of that company. The other was its president.

What Made The Difference?

Have you ever wondered, as I have, what makes this kind of difference in people's lives? It isn't always a native intelligence or talent or dedication. It isn't that one person wants success and the other doesn't.

The difference lies in what each person knows and how he or she makes use of that knowledge.

And that is why I am writing to you and to people like you about The Wall Street

```
Journal. For that is the whole purpose of The
Journal:  To  give  its  readers  knowledge -
knowledge that they can use in business.
```

The last chapter of his classic work, *The Robert Collier Letter Book*, summarized what he saw as the attributes of the ideal sales letter.

Robert Collier was a master psychologist, and since human psychology hasn't changed over the last century, it's no surprise that the advice he offered back in the 1930s is still relevant.

Let's take a peek at what Collier had to tell us and how it applies to our marketing today.

What the Newspaper Editor Told the Cub Reporter

Collier opened his chapter with the story of the newspaper editor advising a cub reporter sent out to cover a wedding.

The editor enumerated the qualities of the ideal wedding that would appeal to tabloid readers: a beautiful heiress eloping with the chauffeur; an irate father with a shotgun and a high-powered car; a smash-up; a heroic rescue; a nip and tuck finish.

The editor advised the reporter to approach the current wedding with this ideal picture in mind, see how many of those dramatic elements he could find, and then build his story around them.

In the same way, Collier said, 'when writing a letter for a product, you should put yourself in the place of your prospective buyer.' Start by thinking of everything that a person could desire in the perfect product. Make a list of the ultimate ideal.

Then, with that in mind, write your letter, focusing on as many features as possible of that ideal version of the product.

On Paint A Truthful Picture

Write your letter in the heat of enthusiasm and excitement, but then it's best to leave it alone for a day so it can cool down, and you can come back to it with fresh, objective eyes. Now you can cross out all the details and descriptions you cannot honestly apply to the product. Don't worry. You'll still have plenty left to say once you've crossed out the excess.

Collier reminds us of the old saying that "there is nothing you can say about a 50-cent cigar that you cannot say about a 5-cent one." Really, the two cigars have basically the same features; the differences are only a matter of degree.

Physically they can be described the same way. The difference in quality will bring a different degree of satisfaction to the smoker. But this is a difference in the *mind* of the smoker only.

Who's to say that a poorer man might not get as much pleasure from his $2 chocolate bar cigar as a rich man does from his $10 chocolate bar? Who is to say that McDonald's isn't as good as any fine dining restaurant? I know plenty of people who would choose McNuggets over a well-cooked steak (myself probably being one of them). The copywriter can paint an equivalent picture of enjoyment for each.

The job of the copywriter is to write descriptions that will build the anticipation of pleasure in the mind's eye of the reader. You never want to exaggerate, or the prospect will disbelieve the whole thing. Especially in today's market where we are exposed to so many sales messages that we can instinctively know when something is true or not. If "something just doesn't' feel right" then your prospective customer will shy away and won't buy.

The writer must create an attractive picture that builds a greater desire for the product than the money the buyer will have to spend.

Collier said it was not necessary to cram every last fact and argument about the product into the letter. However, do pick one critical point on which you think the sale is going to hang, and build the letter around it.

It's also important to add powerful images and arguments that illustrate and support that main argument as your focal point. This will make your letter strong and cohesive, leaving a memorable idea in the mind of your prospect where it can guide his behavior.

On Adding a Sense of Urgency

Just asking for the order is not enough. The ideal sales letter provides a reason why the person must respond at once. It develops a sense of urgency, or as Collier put it, a "Sword of Damocles" hanging over the reader's head.

Put a time limit on the offer. Or explain why supplies are limited and it's first come, first served. Or maybe announce that a price increase will take effect on a specified date. Make it very clear that the opportunity in the offer will be absolutely lost if the reader does not take action within the advertised time limit.

Collier says that ultimately, the most important factor in clinching a sale is the sales letter. While you need a nice envelope, adding an order card, or circular may help. It's the letter that "carries the load." As he puts it, "If you have not the stuff in it, it does not matter where else you have it. It will not do you much good."

To help you write great letters, he suggests keeping an "idea file" with good starters, descriptions, closers, and pointers that you find from other writers. The goal is not to copy them, but to use them for inspiration.

Always remember that "the point that sells your customer is not what your product is, but what it will do for him!"

Also, since the letter will be putting ideas into your reader's head, "be careful not to put in negative ones that you will have to take out again before you can make a sale."

The length of the letter must fit the purpose. If all you want to do is get people to make further inquiries, a short and snappy letter will do nicely. But if you are trying to get someone to commit to a purchase, you need to provide enough information to make that decision.

Tell your story, no matter how long or how short it may be, striving simply to keep it interesting.

On Storytelling

This is my favourite part of marketing. Every brand should be experts in storytelling. Storytelling is what sets the top brans apart from the bottom brands. It's what enables brands to charge more and become more successful.

Although brand storytelling is a relatively new buzzword – it's been around as long as brands have been through the use of inbound and outbound marketing. Brands of all sizes need to hook their customers in through storytelling.

You should think of your own story and the story of your client or company you work for. As a copywriter, you need to think of how do you tell your own brand to your prospective clients.

Storytelling so the perfect platform to let your brand's personality shine through. You need to figure out what your brand story is. It usually involves how the company was formed and what drives the organization. Never be afraid to let your brand's personality come through loud and clear in your storytelling.

For example, storytelling in the automotive industry has been key in marketing campaigns for some time, especially since social media has come on the scene.

Think of it this way: take a step back from your brand and think of your company as the protagonist in some Hollywood movie. What journey has your brand gone one? Where is it going? What is the moral of the story? What are the motifs?

Figuring these questions out will ensure your brand is intrinsically linked to your main messaging.

You should hit them right in the heart. Storytelling in of itself is perhaps the best way to hit that emotional chord with your customers. Tell stories that are real or at the very least based on real stories and tell them in a way that evokes feelings and emotions and so on. Do not under any circumstances try and hit that emotional level just for the sake of hitting it for consumers will see right through you.

Staying fit and maintaining a healthy lifestyle is hard for most people, so a great way to inspire your readers and clients is with stories – people who have succeeded and overcome the challenges. Stories of ordinary people who broke bad habits in extraordinary ways, stories of how we also sometimes feel too lazy or too busy to go to the gym.

Humans have always loved good stories and professional marketers use that fact to their advantage. Do not write fake stories and never claim a story is true that everyone knows is not. I know many famous copywriters have done it in the past, but as I've pointed out before, people are much savvier when it comes to this sort of thing, especially in the digital age where everything and anything is Googleable.

Why do good stories consume us so completely? No other form of writing can keep you up into the wee hours of the night quite like stories. According to research from social psychologists Melanie Green and Timothy Brock, there's a very simple reason why stories are so persuasive: Transportation leads to persuasion. People can block out sales pitches, but everybody loves listening to stories. Their research shows that stories have a tendency to get in "under the radar" and transport us to another place; in this place, we may embrace things we'd likely scoff at in the harsh "real world." This is great news for those adept at telling an enchanting tale, but how can the rest of us write more persuasive stories? According to additional research by the duo, the following tactics work well.

Imagery paints the picture for the story. It's hard to understand how scary Mordor is without Tolkien giving you detailed descriptions of the barren landscapes, the looming presence of Mt. Doom, and the horrifying screams of the Nazgul. Or beloved Hogwarts without the description of the great brick halls, long winding staircases, and large classrooms.

How do you get people to finish a story? Leave them begging to know the end in the very beginning. It's hard for us to not finish things that catch our attention, so lead with something exciting first — not later.

Are You Lowering Your Response Rate?

All brands want high customer retention. And the 'more' can manifest itself in many ways including sales of course but that gets old real fast. A better way to keep them coming back is with storytelling.

When you read a story, not only does the language parts of our brains light up, but any other part of the brain that you would use if you were actually experiencing what we're reading becomes activated as well."

Just consider the fact that Americans alone consumer over 100,000 digital words every single day but 92% say they want brands to tell stories amongst all those words. Don't just throw them boring facts. Tell them a story! Entertain them.

Your sales copy is all carefully designed to bring your prospects to the critical moment where they will pull the trigger and place the order. You don't want to lose them at this point. Your goal is to get them to act in that moment.

But that's just when many marketers make a mistake that actually lowers response to the offer. Marketers become afraid that without a bunch of options their prospect will not buy. I've seen this so many times. The marketer will set up a perfectly good landing page and offer and at the last minute lose their nerve and try to hedge their bets but it only ends up confusing the prospect. In their efforts to make it "easier" on prospects, they offer too many ordering options - and end up driving prospects away.

It's ironic, because you think you're doing the right thing. You want to make people happy. So you offer several different package deals with different price points, several payment programs, a variety of payment options - and you end up with twenty different choices.

You've missed a very important fact: When you have someone interested in your product and ready to order, you want to make it easy on them. Give them too many options and they start thinking too hard. Maybe they're in a hurry and don't have the time to plow through all that information. Or it's just too confusing.

Worst case scenario? They end up putting the whole thing aside, and who knows if they'll ever pick it up again.

If you've been doing this, don't worry. You're not the only one. While it may seem contradictory, it's backed up by psychological research.

Essentially, when the choice got too complicated, people chose not to choose at all. When the choice was easier to deal with, people were more willing to act on their preferences.

These same principles hold true for you as a direct marketer, whether through direct mail or email that leads prospects to a website. It's important to remember that your customer hasn't walked into your store looking for something to buy. You have come into your prospect's home.

You may have gotten prospects to read your sales copy, but you haven't clinched that sale until they actually order. If you demand more of their attention to make a complicated choice, when they really have no basis on which to make it, they could easily lose interest, or even get annoyed, and you've lost a sale you were just about to make.

One of the most successful direct mailings I ever sent was for a client who was a hard-nosed newsletter writer. He wasn't flexible about anything. He only accepted two kinds of credit cards (Visa and Mastercard), he didn't take checks, and he would only sell to people who agreed to sign up for automatic renewal billing every quarter.

Once prospects decided to try his newsletter, their only choice was which of two credit cards to use. That was it. And people signed up like gangbusters. There were no barriers between their decision to buy, and actually buying. It was one simple step to completing the deal.

I recommend you take the same approach with your direct mail or email campaigns for mail order products. Your aim is simply to get people to try one product - not sell them everything in your inventory. Pick your most popular, attractive product - the one that currently has the most sales, and feature that. As far as ordering options, identify the one that most of your customers use now, and narrow your choices down to the ones most likely to be used.

If you are selling some kind of service, or you are a medical professional, select one procedure for an introductory special. Make it the most common procedure that many people start with.

Of course, if you have a store and you want people to come in, they will have access to your entire inventory when they get there. Maybe your best bet there is simply to offer something like a 20% off coupon that they can use on anything they like.

The takeaway here is, once prospects have made the decision to buy, let there be no more complicated decisions for them to make. Always make it easy for prospects to place the order.

On Being Interesting

Stop boring your readers. Everyone has stats, figures and lessons, but you're not writing a textbook. You need to entertain your customers and prospects, otherwise they'll go somewhere else.

What makes this sales letter so effective? It starts with the interesting story. Stories are an amazing way to sell products because they are so memorable. People forget statistics and facts and figures they don't get stories so easily. That is why the fable was created. It is a simple dramatized way to show people the benefits of meeting the Journal.

The other factor is the strong use of fear to motivate somebody to. Nobody likes to be left behind or left out. Fear is by far the strongest way to motivate anybody into doing anything. By showing that doing nothing is more harmful than acting is always the best way to sell something.

It also layers in the facts and the fits of reading the Wall Street Journal. For example, you become smarter, more business savvy, and more informed.

Then there is a great call to action which is repeated in two different ways and a strong guarantee. "GREAT INTRODUCTORY PRICE!" Now who wouldn't want a special price? When you doing your sales letters think of a great offer, discount, or special price that you can offer them. YOu also have to love the PS "The journals subscription price may be tax deductible." It just adds an extra bonus on top of the bonus.

Gary Hulbert believed that not only studying successful ads writing them down by hand, word for word, is the best way to develop his or her craft. Many of his students who tried this method did go on to become great copywriters. This may seem an old-fashioned way of learning but even when you write something down there something in your brain that is triggered that helps you remember it. When I take notes even if I don't refer back to my notes I remember what I wrote down better than if I had just listened. It seems that doing this exercise helps in remembering the great ads.

When you first start an email campaign or direct mail piece you want to take a look at all the people you will be contacted. This list is carefully selected to contain the names of individuals who have either brought your products in the past, and interested in them, or have bought something similar.

Do not send your campaign to people who have no interest in your product or service. It is acceptable to send a mail piece to homes in your area if your furniture store for example. Every home meets furniture and has bought furniture in the past. But don't send the same people the piece promoting a CRM system. A CRM system is only good for business owners you don't know if they are even interested. This is called spam you want to avoid it if at all possible. Spamming some people occasionally is just a part of marketing but don't be malicious about it.

You want to find out as much you can about these people. If they are in an email marketing software and they likely have demographic and psychographics. These are useful to get to know your audience. If they're not in any sort of system and are just a list of names that look at the information you have. What area do they live in Mark's upscale downscale? Do they live in the countryside or in big cities? Do they live in apartments or multifamily homes? Are they Asian or Caucasian?

You can tell a lot about your target market just by some simple guesswork. If you have the phone numbers of your customers you should try contacting them and talking to them. You can get some really great information about them this way that will be effective. This is kind of like a mini focus group with your target market. I know this can get very uncomfortable since not a lot of people like phoning up complete strangers and asking them questions but it will really help your marketing. Another way of using the phone effectively is to follow up with a sales team after he sent out your direct mail piece. Remember it often takes five touches on more for a customer to buy from you so don't be afraid of reaching out to them in different ways.

On Long Versus Short

This is the eternal struggle in advertisement especially now that you are ads can be unlimited without any extra cost on the web. This battle is like the epic one between climate change camps. Which is better short ads or long? Nobody can say definitively and it varies from ad to ad and industry to industry. However to make a case here that long is generally better than short.

You hear many marketers saying that in today's social media world, you only have a couple of seconds to grab their attention and convert them to customers. You will capture more people's attention with a short snappy ad.

While this may be true, people looking to buy actually want to know all the facts and details they don't mind watching a 10-minute video or reading several pages of content about something they want to buy. Think about the last major purchasing decision you made.

How long did you take to research and come to a decision? I remember when I was researching a new phone read everything and watched everything I could about that phone. I found the reviews compared it to other phones and sought out everybody's opinion. I gathered as much data as I could. This is generally the case with more expensive products as well.

Craig Simpson the owner of Simpson Direct Inc. worked for a client who was sending out a 36-page sales letter. The letter was lengthy, poorly written, and repetitive. According to Simpson, reading it felt like slogging through a large swampland, just to get to the meat and bones of the product. They decided to take the letter up to a 24-page piece. They removed the bad grammar and the repetition and as a result, the whole piece flowed much better. Even though they knew they had a winner, Craig was not so egotistical just to toss out the old. Instead, he tested the shorter version with the longer and to his surprise, he found that the 36 pages had double the response rate as his you are version.

Again, it goes to show that you should test everything, no matter how much you think you know. Create two versions of the same ad copy and test them to see which one works better. It never hurts to go longer because there will always be a place for it, even if it doesn't perform well in your usual channels.

On Old School Mail

Depending on your market and who you're trying to target, might be beneficial to go back to old-school mailing. Why? Because everyone is used to being bombarded on the internet but very few people are getting mail anymore and if you are able to get people's attention through the mailbox, then they can be even more powerful than something on the web.

It can actually be an extremely powerful tool. And uou won't know until you try it, right? I've run quit a few successful mailer campaigns in different industries and each time I had the attitude that this is never going to work. Was I ever wrong!

If you do it, then you want to do it right. Don't just put it in an ordinary envelope with your logo on top. That signifies junk mail if I ever saw it. First Class mail gets noticed and respected a lot more than regular mail. This is not only a cue for your prospects but also for the carrier as well. It may be a little bit more expensive but it's also going to get noticed more. Besides, there is nothing more expensive than advertising that doesn't work. Anything you do to make your sales letter look more like First Class mail the more it's going to be delivered and opened and read.

Use personalized stamps instead of a postage meter. Again I know this can be a pain and I know if you are sending out thousands of letters and this may not be practical, but I would encourage you if there's a prospect at you have been trying to reach forever and would be a game changer to your business then why not try it? A person I stamp will be noticed by your prospect and much more likely to be opened.

Sometimes we're happy with our sales piece. Perhaps we put a lot of effort into creating and testing it, and at this point, we don't want to change it, but we wonder if there are other things we can do to increase the response to our campaigns.

The return address that says acne marketing Co. is obviously an ad and will send alarm bells off in your prospect. Remember people are desperately trying not to be advertised. Today people get thousands of marketing messages a day thrown at them and the only way our brain can deal with them is by shutting them out.

However, a classy-looking return address that gives street address with no name could be anything and it arises curiosity. Gary Halbert did this with great effect when he rented a mailbox in Beverly Hills. He would sign all of his mail with a Beverly Hills return address. Not only did the most famous ZIP Code get people's attention but it also increased his authority. (If he's living in Beverly Hills, he must know what he's talking about, right?)

Try Not Putting Teaser Copy On The Envelope

Teaser copy is another red flag that this is an ad trying to sell you something. A plain envelope could be a letter from a friend or an invitation. It's left to the imagination of the prospect as to what is inside. The more curious you can make the prospect the better. This is especially good for new prospects that you haven't formed a relationship with yet. Whatever you do, you should test everything yourself and see how it works.

Print the word **"RUSH"** in red on the envelope. This arouses curiosity and adds a sense of urgency, strengthening the illusion that this is a first-class letter.

You can try using first-class postage. In some cases, an increased response may make it worthwhile to send letters first class. You'll have to work out the cost-benefit analysis for yourself.

Another advantage of mailing first class is that you get undelivered mail returned to you, which allows you to clean up your mailing list for future campaigns. And if your list broker and mail house know you're keeping a "nixie" file (i.e., of returned/undeliverable mail), they're more likely to give you clean lists and sterling service.

Online applications

You can adapt these techniques for use in emails as well.

- Have it come from an email address that sounds classy. Use personalization in the subject line and on the email itself, e.g., "Dear Greg."

- Use a subject line that makes it sound like there is important information in the email.
- Lead with news in the subject line, especially if you're emailing to your own list.

Make Physical Changes to the Letter

Now that you've made the envelope (or your subject line) more appealing so that prospects will open it, there are things you can do to the letter itself that will make them want to read it. These can also apply to the layout of your email, webpage, or job application.

Make the letter easier on the eyes. Provide "eye relief" so the letter doesn't look so formidable. By setting it up correctly, you can make the letter inviting so that prospects will want to read it.

For example:

- Keep margins wide and the typeface easy to read.
- Use lots of subheads that break up the text.
- Highlight some of the copy by making it bold, or another color.
- Make it look like it would be fun to read.

Add a photo of the signer of the letter. People like to see whom they're dealing with. If they see a picture of the person who is promising to teach them how to make a fortune or train their dog, they feel they have a more personal connection. For online applications, if you're using HTML format, you can put a photo of the signer above the fold.

Put your phone number in the body copy of your letter (or email, etc.)

Also, invite prospects to call you with any questions. A prominent phone number and invitation to call builds confidence that you are a legitimate business that cares about making your buyers happy. It makes people feel safe, and the safer they feel, the more likely they are to place an order.

Improve Your Guarantee

Every offer should have a guarantee. This eases prospects' concerns and makes responses seem less risky. If you're giving just a 30-day or 60-day guarantee, consider raising it to a full year. Not only does this increase response rates, but it reduces returns as people become less likely to return the product as more time passes.

Rent a More Responsive Mailing List

Research shows the most important factor in the success of any direct mail or email campaign is the mailing list. If your campaigns are failing, the first thing to do is look at finding a new mailing list. Always keep accurate records of how well or poorly lists do and get rid of the duds.

And There's More . . .

Halbert had other suggestions. For example, some post offices are more efficient than others, so try mailing from several different ones. Also, some letter shops do a better job than others, so test those out as well. Online, you might experiment with emailing from multiple IP addresses.

Always Work to Find a Better Way

There's no end to the changes we can make in the way we present our message so we get a better response. Don't ever stop trying something new because you think what you're doing is "good enough." Just one small change could add a huge boost to the effectiveness of your campaign.

Chapter: Ten:

On SEO Copy

Don't confuse visibility with credibility.

-Harvey Mackay

Content marketing or Search Engine Optimization (SEO for short) has been all the rage for the last twenty years or so, but it's actually an old form of marketing. In fact, it's actually been around for more than 100 years!

This medium is about supplying your prospects and customers with information that doesn't specifically sell the product or service you offer. It is like a bonus or gift you provide free of charge.

It's effective whether your business is web-based or brick and mortar. But how does it work? And is it worth your time?

I have been doing a lot of SEO copywriting for the last five or six years and I can for certain say YES! It does work. In fact, all my clients as I'm writing this, are currently on the first page of Google for their keywords and enjoy the traffic and the sales that comes along with it.

When I was working in the cannabis space, SEO and email marketing were the only marketing venues that actually worked. Every other type of avenue blocked us from promoting our product and so we spent a shit tone of money on optimized content. Guess what? It worked because people were interested in learning about the different aspects of the cannabis plant. (It is fascinating by the way. I learned a lot too.)

Content marketing provides many advantages. First off, it establishes a relationship with your prospects. It cultivates warm feelings, product or company loyalty, and a sense that your business is a valuable resource to the person. It shows you in a very favorable light and it keeps positive attention on your product.

These friendly associations build your value in prospects' eyes - the more so because you don't seem to be asking anything of them. You appear to be just generously giving something away.

On Content Marketing History

Although Search Engine Optimization is a relatively new field, content marketing, on the other hand, has been around a long time. One of the first users (at least according to marketing history) of content marketing was August Oetker, who manufactured baking powder in the late 1800s. In 1891 he started printing recipes on the back of his packages, which became quite popular.

In 1911 he started publishing and giving away a stand-alone cookbook. This cookbook had a global reach to millions of consumers and are still extremely popular today. When these home cooks went to the store to buy ingredients, they naturally reached for Dr. Oetker's products.

By investing in publishing and giving away cookbooks, Oetker created a loyal customer base that likely extended over generations of family members. Many food companies copied this brilliant idea by also providing recipes for free. Today, cooks all over America have cookbooks on their shelves from Hershey's, Jell-O, Bisquik, Pace Foods, and countless others.

In 1895, John Deere became one of the first companies to provide an ongoing magazine for customers when it started publishing *The Furrow*. Now you probably receive a number of magazines from companies and organizations you do business with, like insurance companies, vitamin stores, and the American Automobile Association. You can thank John Deere for that.

The world-famous *Michelin Guide* was first published in 1900 as a free gift to customers - although it became so big they eventually started charging for their informative tour guides.

Every time customers look up a recipe in a cookbook, watch a Youtube tutorial, or read interesting articles online or in a magazine, the company that provided material gets priceless positive attention. And those publications can hang around someone's home for years, multiplying their value. This is why content marketing is such a great way to stretch your advertising budget.

If you're thinking a publication is expensive to create, print, and distribute, consider you are both right and wrong. It does take a lot of sweat equity to create content and you have to be patient but it is well worth it. If you consider that in many industries, it costs around five dollars a click to advertise on Google — that's five dollars just for the privilege of visiting your website, creating and distributing content doesn't sound so bad. Those who do it well are patient and they understand the long term payoff.

Today many marketers put their content online which cuts down on costs considerably. They keep a regular, highly information blog, maybe send prospects to a free report or an interactive website of some sort. Customers are delighted with the information - at little cost to the company.

On Endless Possibilities

No matter what business you're in, there is some form of information you can provide that would be valuable to your customers. Here are some suggestions:

How-to guides are always welcome. These could be directions for using your product or different ways to use it. If you own a home construction firm, you might provide a home-decorating guide, a list of rules for selecting paint colors or flooring or counter materials, or how to talk to a contractor (with a glossary of construction terms).

A CPA could provide a guide to different investment instruments, a guide to organizing tax materials, or a guide for determining how much income will be required for a comfortable lifestyle in retirement. A print shop could offer a pamphlet on paper and ink choices, different types of business cards, and fonts that are best for different uses. A wedding planner could be a great gift to couples buying wedding invitations.

Any business could provide handouts with 'Frequently Asked Questions', trouble-shooting directions, brochures on equipment or services, calendars, etc.

Consider writing something called a "white paper," which is an extended report on some aspect of your business. For example, if you're a doctor, you could create a series of white papers on different kinds of medical procedures or conditions.

Sometimes the information provided could just be fun. Stock publications are available with jokes, trivia, and human-interest stories that any company can buy, imprint with their own name, and then distribute to all its customers. It may have nothing to do with anything the company offers. It's just a gift.

Effective SEO copywrites tell Google which words are the most relevant ones and the ones people want to reach. You don't necessarily have to fully optimize your landing page copy up front, but you need to begin with the end in mind from a keyword standpoint.

The beauty of building a reader-focused online presence based on valuable content is that you can do well even if Google changes its algorithms simply by getting people to opt-in and follow you over time. Google's main objective is to provide value to its customers (the people searching) and if you continue to do that, Google will ensure your page is ranked high, even if it's not stuffed with keywords or backlinks.

Part of being SEO friendly content is to use language in your content that is relevant to searches and language they are also using. That's where keyword research comes in.

The essential elements of search engine keyword research is that it allows you to gaze directly into your prospect's minds and figure out how they think and type. Look at the actual phrases and words they used to find information. There are a lot of great tools out there to help you with this including SEMrush, Moz and SE Ranking. If you don't want to spend money, there is also a Chrome extension, Keyword.io, and, of course, Google Ads Keyword Planner.

Once complete, you get an excellent idea of the words people most often use when thinking and searching for a certain topic. Once armed with keyword intelligence that's relevant to your niche, you have the unique ability to create highly relevant content that aids your site visitors and enhances your credibility. You're speaking the language of the audience and satisfying their needs – which is what great SEO is all about. If you do this correctly you'll rank high after promoting the content and gaining traffic from social media.

Once armed with keyword intelligence that's relevant to your niche, you have the unique ability to create highly relevant content that aids your site visitors and enhances your credibility. You're speaking the language of the audience, and satisfying their needs. And if you get it right, you'll likely rank well in search engines too – after promoting the content and gaining traffic from social media. It may seem strange to view search traffic as a secondary benefit in a Google-driven world, but that's exactly how you should view it.

Google won't treat you as relevant until others do first. It's a bit like the cart before the horse but that's the game we play.

The counterintuitive rule of search engine keyword research is to try to forget that search engines can send you traffic. View the data as free or low-cost market research and you'll have the proper mindset to formulate a content strategy that has a shot at ranking well. People need to like your content before Google will.

Here are five essential things to understand when it comes to keyword research:

1. **Research Tools:** There are tons of free and paid tools out there. I use the Google Keyword planner but you might find one that better fits your needs. Whatever one you choose, don't take it as gospel. These tools are just like everything else: you need to test them against actual results.

2. **Get Specific:** "Keyword" is the term that gets tossed around, but what you really want in most cases are keyword phrases, also know as long-tail-keyword phrases. An example of this would be "Los Angeles Indian beauty salon". These are more specific than "beauty salon" and target the people who you want. A note of warning here. You don't want to stuff your copy with awkward keywords or keyword phrases so they sound unnatural. Not only will it turn off your readers but Google is smart enough to realize that you're trying to game the system and won't like you either.

3. **Strength in Numbers:** As mentioned before, don't take as gospel truth the reported number of monthly searches provided by any particular tool. But do pay attention to relative popularity among search terms. You want to make sure enough people use that phrase when thinking of your niche to make it worth your while, especially if this is one of the primary search terms you want to target for your site overall. At the same time, be realistic. If you are trying to rank in a very competitive sector, make sure that a certain keyword combination can rank for an easier phrase if the more competitive term ends up out of reach.

4. **Highly Relevant:** Make sure that the search terms you are considering are highly relevant to your ultimate goal. If you're a service provider or selling specific products, keyword relevancy may be easier to determine — you ultimately want someone to purchase the product or service. Other goals may require more careful

consideration, such as subscriptions to content publications and contributions to charities, for example.

5. **Develop a Content Resource On Your Website:** Can a particular keyword phrase support the development of content that is a valuable resource to readers and act as a foundational element of what your business is about? Something that: Satisfies the preliminary needs of the site visitor Acts as the first step in your sales or action cycle Prompts people to link to it It's this step 5 – a foundational content resource – that translates keyword research into strong search rankings, so we're going to look at it in more detail next.

6. **Backlinks:** These are when somebody links to your website and one of the top factors in how Google ranks your content. These are incredibly valuable to your website. But how can you control them? First off, make sure your website is listed in all the relevant directories. Do you work for a restaurant? Make sure it's listed on Yelp and Foursquare. Research forums in your industry. If people are posting questions on Reddit and Quora about your industry be sure to answer them and link back to your website. Then, of course, you can always ask other bloggers in your industry to link back to your website. You can always do a link exchange or guest blog on their site. This is obviously a huge topic by itself and one we will revisit later in this chapter.

How To Create Cornerstone Content That Google Loves

Imagine for a second, someone has just arrived at your website, and this person has no idea what you're website is trying to convey. Imgine that this is an important visitor, your idea customer just waiting to buy. Pretend further that this single visitor could make the difference between success and failure for your business. He or she has no time to waste poking around your site trying to figure out what you're all about, so she immediately picks up the phone and calls you, demanding an explanation.

What do you tell him or her? You'd probably give her essential information about how you understand her problem, options for solving the problem etc. Examples of how you can help, and explanations of why you perfectly meet her needs, right? And I'm betting you'd want to explain it in the most compelling fashion you could, given what's riding on the deal.

In a nutshell, that's what Google wants you to do with the content on your site. When trying to rank well for the central topics your site is built around, creating cornerstone content is your best bet. Whether it's extended tutorials about keyword research, content marketing, or copywriting, a unique frequently asked questions page, or an inspirational mission statement, this content serves a vital function in creating a relevant, compelling, and useful cornerstone that provides your site with a solid foundation for search optimization and usability.

A cornerstone is something that is basic, essential, indispensable, and the chief foundation upon which something is built. It's what people need to know to make use of your website and do business with you. And when approached in a strategic fashion, this content can rank extremely well in search engines. The key is creating compelling content that's worth linking to, and then finding a way to get the word out.

When you build your blog you want to have maybe 10 cornerstone pieces which should be between 5,000 and 10,000 words and before you start yelling at me – YOU WANT ME TO DO WHAT NOW?? – keep in mind that you are competing against tens if not hundreds of thousands of blogs; yours needs to be better and more valuable. In between these cornerstone pieces, you can write smaller pieces that go into detail about some aspect of your business that isn't covered off in the cornerstone pieces. Then make sure to connect the relevant blogs together with links.

Think of the business as the tree trunk, the foundation, and your cornerstone content as the thick branches and then the rest of your blogs as the branches.

As mentioned, the first goal of cornerstone content is obviously usefulness and relevancy to the website visitor, no matter how they arrive. (I'll only hit you over the head with this fact a couple more times!) The second goal is to make that content so compelling and comprehensive that people are willing – no, make that excited – to link to it.

We now know the real secret to modern SEO is creating content that naturally attracts links, rather than begging for links to crummy keyword-stuffed web pages. In other words, SEO copywriting is now all about response-oriented, high-value copy — concepts and words that ultimately result in a favorable action from the reader. Since the popularity of our content depends so much on what people do off the page, it makes sense that we might also need to step outside the confines of the page itself to get the word out. Luckily, the same copywriting skills you use to conceive and create your content applies to promoting it as well.

The way to create compelling content is to focus relentlessly on "what's in it for the reader." And in the same way, no one is going to link to you unless there's something in it for them. The key is the same — understand who you're talking to, figure out what will catch their attention, then convince them to take the action you want.

Now, taking into account what we know about keyword research, choose the most appropriate keyword phrase for your content. In other words, what is the relevant question searchers are asking that your content and business solution answer? Will answering that question aid a visitor to your site in getting the most out of the experience? Are enough people asking that question to make ambitiously answering it worthwhile? Then you have to make sure that search engines think your content is actually about that keyword or combination of keywords. We'll get to that shortly.

No one in the SEO field disputes the importance of using your targeted keyword phrase in your title tag. Search engines want to offer relevant results, so those results should prominently reflect the words the searcher is using in the title of the page. But also remember, the title tag is a headline.

You want to speak back to the prospective reader in her own chosen words. Plus, you want to wrap those words in a compelling headline structure that promises to answer the exact question the searcher is asking with the query. And finally, writing a killer keyword-enhanced headline makes it more likely that someone will simply use your title to link back to you. Since link anchor text is a significant component of search engine algorithms, putting the right keywords into your headline can give your content a significant boost.

Longer Vs. Shorter Revisited

Remember that conversation we had about longer vs. shorter. Well, it turns out longer wins out in SEO content as well. It seems articles over 2,000 words are the sweet spot, although I would push you to write over 5,000 words.

That means your content has to be impressive, both in quality and scope. You can develop an awesome multi-part tutorial or write an inspirational manifesto. Answer the question so much better and more comprehensively than the competition does, and chances are much better that your effort becomes worth linking to and your search results improve dramatically.

If you're going to be ambitious in scope with your content, it makes sense to make things easy on the reader from a usability standpoint. A content landing page is designed to instantly communicate what's going on to the visitor as soon as they arrive, and also acts as a table of contents (via links to each part of the tutorial) that increases clarity. Here are some of the benefits of the content landing page approach:

Keeping a reader from hitting the back button is crucial to just about every aspect of successful cornerstone content. You can't score a reader, customer, or link if the benefit of the resource is not quickly communicated.

Having said that, can a 500-word article still rank well for a competitive search term all by itself? It can be difficult but not impossible. Sometimes you just get lucky with your content and you manage to leapfrog over other blog posts. It all depends on the competition.

On Bookmarks and Sharing

When presented with a highly beneficial (if somewhat overwhelming) multi-part resource, the first impulse is often to bookmark the page for a return visit.

When that bookmarking occurs at a social site like Delicious, Pinterest, or StumbleUpon, Scoop.it it can lead to long-term traffic. And don't forget that sharing killer content is a sign of social media status among influencers.

Content landing pages help you score the bookmark and prompt that sharing impulse at a glance. Likewise, a visiting blogger or webmaster might be instantly impressed with your work, and link to you based on the benefits and scope communicated by the landing page itself. The quicker you can impress a potential link source, the easier you're making it for them to follow through.

Search engines favor websites that have a lot of relevant, frequently-updated content, and they also like a lot of general link authority. Given how easy it is to publish blogs, it's smart to use tools and software to manage all that content. And given that active blogging allows for constant participation in the social media space, it's a critical way to build general site authority via links, delve into specific and related topics, and to reference your cornerstone content.

You also might consider putting a link to your essential content in your site sidebar. If you've focused on the right topics, you'll naturally keep cross-referencing your cornerstone content and link to it from your future content as well. SEO copywriting is now all about response-oriented copy – concepts and words that ultimately result in a favorable action from the reader.

Don't go overboard, but do provide context when discussing advanced topics that require an understanding of the basics. Never assume that everyone is aware of your cornerstone resource or understands the basics. Periodically linking to your cornerstone content lets it find new readers — and fresh links.

On Guest Blogging

Guest writing on established blogs and other content sites has become the most powerful strategy for getting your own site rolling. You freely contribute content that not only allows you to raise your profile but allows for links back to your own site. Once again, creating killer original content will open doors for you, especially when it's created for the benefit of someone else. And you can use that killer cornerstone content you've already produced as an example of the quality you can deliver.

Depending on your relationship with the site owner, you may be able to link to your cornerstone content from within the body of the content itself, but only if the citation is extremely relevant to the content and beneficial to the reader. Otherwise, your link needs to go in your byline or bio.

Most people tend to link to their site or blog URL in the byline of contributed content. Turn it around by focusing the byline on the reader instead of yourself, and feature your cornerstone content instead of your home page. For example, if I were to guest blog somewhere about strategies for attracting links, which byline is more attractive to the reader when finishing my article?

Not only is that better for the reader, it's better for you. Your link helps your cornerstone content rank higher for a popular search term. Just be careful about using the same anchor text over and over, as this can send the wrong signal to Google.

Social Networking platforms like 'Twitter', 'LinkedIn,' and 'Facebook' have become amazing content distribution networks. Remember, gaining followers and fans is not about your ego, it's about creating a dynamic network which results in new people seeing your content. And the more people see and share your content, the more likely it is to attract those valuable links. But it's not really about one-off link requests.

Social media is about establishing and growing 30 relationships with influencers online. These are the prominent bloggers in your niche, top users, relevant web journalists, and social media mavens. You need to network from a "what's in it for them" perspective. Catch attention, gain interest, and create a desire to help you in the future by offering something that benefits them first.

You should engage with the owners or staff of content sites relevant to your niche. Comment on their blogs, tweet them, email them. It is a great way to get noticed, and it can lead to links back to you. Bloggers definitely watch who is linking to them, and you can take the initiative by linking out first before looking for a link in return. Simply linking out for the sake of linking won't accomplish much, especially with bloggers who receive lots of links.

The key is to be strategic about how you link and what you say. It's just like any other conversation. Join in and add your two cents, but make sure you've got something substantive to say that will reflect well on you. Use a great headline to make sure you are noticed, and then deliver the 31 goods. And since your cornerstone content is the foundation of what the conversation is likely about, finding a way to mention it in the context of the dialogue will naturally bring it to the attention of influencers in your field.

The words you put on a web page have no life of their own until they get read. And those same words will not gain prominence in search engines until the words are linked to by relevant, authoritative sources.

Google can still be gamed to a degree, just like offline organizations and systems can be exploited. However, the goals of the search engines are similar to society at large, and they are getting very good at finding rule breakers and dispensing swift punishment. Creating compelling content and beneficial relationships are link attraction strategies that won't get you banned or penalized.

You're also simultaneously achieving your overall goal of converting site visitors into customers, clients, revenue and profits. Now it's time to turn to the "last mile" of search engine optimization – the location and frequency of keywords in your "on-page" copy, and other SEO best practices that help you outrank the competition.

If you have a good website that is useful, relevant and easy to crawl, you will get good SEO but the right search traffic – targeted towards the right people – doesn't just happen, not unless you're lucky (which simply means you don't know what you're doing).

Here are five things that make your content easy to digest for search engines so you can rank as well as possible. Whether you optimize up front or later, you at minimum need to know what keywords you're targeting and include them in the title of your content. It's generally accepted that the closer to the front of the title your keywords are, the better. But the key is that they appear in the title somewhere. It's important that your CMS or blogging software allows you to serve an alternate title in the title tag (which is the snippet of code Google pulls to display a title in search results) than the headline that appears on the page.

If you use WordPress, Genesis builds this and many other SEO functions directly into your posting interface, in addition to all its design controls. Let's say I decide that the most compelling headline for prompting readership, sharing, and linking for an article is: "Five

Areas to Focus On for Effective SEO Copywriting." That title contains my keyword phrase (SEO copywriting), but they might not be in the best location for ranking or even for quick-scanning searchers compared with regular readers. By using an alternate title tag, I can enter a more search-optimized title for Google and searchers only.

The emphasis on keywords in the title makes practical sense from a search engine standpoint. When people search for something, they're going to want to see the language they used reflected back at them in the results. Nothing mysterious about that. 35 Having keywords in your title is also important when people link to you.

When your keywords are there, people are more likely to link to you with the keywords in the anchor text. This is an important factor for Google to determine that a particular page is in fact about a particular subject. You should try to keep the length of your title under 72 characters for search purposes. This will ensure the full title is visible in a search result, increasing the likelihood of a click-through.

Meta Description SEO copywriting is not just about ranking. It's also about what your content looks like on a search engine results page. The meta description of your content will generally be the "snippet" copy for the search result below the title, which influences whether or not you get the click.

Keywords in your meta description don't directly influence rank, but it doesn't matter. What it does is it provides a better user experience for your potential customer and that is something search engines love! You want to lead off your meta description with the keyword phrase and succinctly summarize the page as a reassurance to the searcher that your content will satisfy what they're looking for. Try to keep the meta description under 165 characters so the full description is visible in the search result. Again, you can create a meta description in WordPress right in the posting area with Genesis and other themes and plugins that add SEO functionality.

Content Unique and frequently-updated content makes search engines happy, but you know that. For search optimization purposes (and just general reader friendliness) your content should be tightly on-topic and strongly centered on the subject matter of the desired keyword phrases.

It's generally accepted that very brief content may have a harder time ranking over a page with more substantial content so you'll want to have a content body length of at least 500 words. It might also help to bold or italicize the first occurrence of a keyword phrase, or include it in a bulleted list, but I usually don't get hung up on that. It's also debatable whether including keywords in subheads helps with ranking, but again, it doesn't matter – subheads are simply a smart and natural place to include your keyword phrase, since that's what the page (and each section) is about.

On Keywords

Keyword frequency is the number of times your targeted keyword phrase appears on the page. Keyword density is the ratio of those keywords to the rest of the words on the page. It's generally accepted that keyword frequency affects ranking (and that makes logical sense). Keyword density, as some sort of "golden" ratio, does not. But the only way to make sense of an appropriate frequency is via the ratio of those keywords to the rest of the content, so density is still a metric you should pay attention to. In other words, the only way to tell if your repetition of keywords is super or spammy is to measure that frequency against the overall length of the content. A keyword density greater than 5.5% could find you guilty of what's called keyword stuffing, which tends to make Google think you're trying to game them. Bad idea. Just keep in mind that you don't need to mindlessly repeat keywords to optimize. In fact, if you do, you'll probably get the opposite result.

On Links

As mentioned, outbound links are the fundamental basis of the web. Search engines want to know you're sufficiently "connected" with other pages and content, so linking out to other pages matters when it comes to search engine optimization.

Here are some rules of thumb for linking based on generally accepted best practices:

- Link to relevant content early in the body copy.

- Link to relevant interior pages of your site or other sites

- Link with naturally relevant anchor text Again, these are guidelines related to current best practices.

Don't get hung up on rules; focus on the intent behind what search engines are looking for – giving those human searchers quality results.

Does writing for people work for SEO? Hang around web writing circles for any length of time, and the inevitable "write for the bots or write for people" debate comes up. Last time I checked, it's people who use search engines, not some other life form. So you're always writing for people. Obviously, the debate stems from the fact that search engines are powered by computer algorithms. But as search engines have gotten smarter, writing that pleases people and satisfies the bots is not that far apart, if at all. Let's look at four factors which work well for SEO and see how well they cater to the needs of people.

As we saw earlier, link attraction is the biggest aspect of today's practice of search engine optimization. Google looks at the links pointing at your domain — and those pointing at particular pages — as votes of legitimacy.

Google also takes into account the words people use when linking to you (anchor text) to get an idea of what the right keywords would be for your page. While it's still possible to buy links (not what we'd advise), there's no way to "trick" someone into linking to you. People link because there's something in it for them in some way, and because something about your content compels them to do it.

The smartest SEO strategists create valuable content because it answers questions people are seeking. Last time I checked, it's human beings who use search engines, not some other life form. So you're always writing for people. Because Google has tons of information thanks to Google Advertising (formally Google Adwords), Google Console, Google Analytics, Tool Bar and Website Optimizer, some see search algorithms moving away from links and more to site usage data (how people actually interact with content). Whether that's the case or not, content that people find compelling will continue to constitute the biggest factor in search engine optimization.

One smart strategy for content marketing and anyone building an authority site is to create valuable content resources related to the most important topics you discuss. As you know, I call this cornerstone content, because it's the fundamental information your site is built on. This directs the majority of links to that page instead of the individual parts and allows for easy cross-linking in future content. It also prompts social bookmarking and sharing due to the scope of the resource. But the real reason it works is because it's people-friendly. Given the usual scattered, backward-chronological nature of a blog, the page is highly usable and useful as a resource for people new to copywriting (and for those who want to link to a resource about copywriting).

Speaking the language of the audience. Whether Google moves more to usage data over links as an indicator of quality remains to be seen. But one song remains the same – Google has to match up what a page is about with what people are searching for. That means your words need to match up with the way searchers most like to talk about your topic.

Anyone who's not interested in understanding and mirroring the language used by their intended audience is simply not interested in being an effective communicator, search engine traffic or not. As I've said, telling search engines that what you're talking about is the same as what people are looking for is the essence of SEO. But even if search engines didn't deliver traffic at all, the ability to know, understand, and mirror the language of the audience is an amazing gift we've been given thanks to search data. Why not use it when people respond well to it?

Good SEO makes content more readable. Don't just barf up a bunch of text on the page and expect people to read it. Use graphics, bold text, and shorter paragraphs.

When you implement the whole range of SEO best practices, you rank well with reader-friendly content (that's why it got links in the first place). We've talked about keyword stuffing so we don't go into too much detail here. However, it's true that you can underuse keywords in relation to the overall length of the content, hurting your ranking potential. But most people new to SEO copywriting tend to overuse keywords beyond what's necessary. The myth that search optimized content is ugly and unreadable is simply that – a myth. Especially nowadays. When you approach SEO copywriting in a logical, informed fashion, your content isn't keyword stuffed. It's natural, and compelling, and artful.

At this point, I hope you have a better feel and understanding of the modern practice of SEO copywriting. But it can still be a little overwhelming, especially in the context of the balancing act that is your business. Given the demand for loads of fresh, compelling content combined with the need to carefully optimize for search engines, the sheer volume of new content coming out each day, quality modern SEO copywriting is critical for website owners and even bigger business for professional web writers.

Think About What's Possible Online

When you think about SEO content, you don't just have to think about blog articles. With fast-loading mobile phones and wi-fi everywhere, the possibilities of SEO content are indeed endless.

Interactive sites are very appealing. Quizzes and games are fun. But you can also have helpful tools. For example, if you sell paint, you can have standard pictures of houses that prospects can "paint" different colors. Or a medical office can have people go through a symptom tree to help diagnose an illness, or see if symptoms are severe enough to warrant an office visit.

Give it some thought and you may come up with many great ideas for getting people to your site. Providing something valuable to them will establish a relationship - and chances increase that they will come to you the next time they need your product or service.

A Few Things NOT To Do...

The whole point of your content marketing is to reflect well on your business and ultimately increase sales, so don't provide content that will interfere with these aims.

First, make sure your information is appropriate for your business and customers. If you run a funeral parlor, it's best to stay away from humor. If you provide home remodeling for houses in the $500,000 range, don't provide information appropriate for houses in the $200,000 range or the $2,000,000 range. Only provide what will be seen as valuable to your target audience. This may seem like common sense but you'd be surprised at how often this simple rule gets overlooked.

Secondly, make sure your information doesn't look like a poorly disguised ad. Make sure the information is valuable in and of itself, and isn't just a sales pitch for you.

On Make It All Work Together

SEO copywriting has become more complicated over the last years as Google algorithms have changed and become smarter. No longer can you stuff your content with the relevant keywords and have it appear on the first page. Is no doubt that the location and frequency of keywords are still important however Google tries to match up the most relevant content for the people searching it.

Ultimately if your content is unreadable, it will rank lower than something people find interesting and engaging, which is how it should be. Nobody knows the true algorithm of Google, not even the people who work there. The algorithm is created by hundreds of people who put their own little spin on things so it is impossible for one company one person to know everything. We can only take our best guess and listen to what the people at Google say.

A good SEO copyrighter is primarily a smart content creator. He or she has the knack for tuning the needs and desires of the prospects audience into compelling content. And because links and social sharing are so important, the needs and desires have to be nailed well before the content will show up prominently in the search engines.

The same emotional forces and psychology that prompt people to buy can also be the ones cause people to link back to a blog or a website. Always, always, always ask yourself what creates the most value for your reader.

Algorithms will be continued to be updated and changed and perhaps it will still be possible to game the system find a loophole that you can exploit but in the long term, the best strategy is to think about your customers and how best to serve them.

Many firms and companies these days are hiring people out of India or China to write for SEO purposes otherwise known as content farms. Although content farming is not as popular as it once was, it still happens. However, it would be more effective to flush your money down the drain and hire a content farmer. I'm not just saying this for my own benefit but it's true. No content is better than terrible content.

Google will eventually sniff this content out and will value them very low, if at all. If you can come up with a fresh way of doing things written smartly and you are going to be in high demand.

I would encourage you to write one good piece of content than for mediocre pieces. Take your time to bring your unique perspective to the problem and find a solution do not just copy what somebody else has already done that is pointless It may seem like a lot of work for only about a third of the payoff but you need a way to sift through the minutia.

Great pieces of writing will be liked shared and read for years to come. The great thing about ideas and writing is that it never gets old. I've just updated this in a second edition and I have a feeling there will be many more editions to come. We are still reading books that have been written 2,000 years ago.

The copyrighter will be a vital and well-rounded part of any marketing effort. Using the power of social media to gain exposure for the content will result in natural links and signals of quality and relevance. Focusing on enhancing the natural authority of a website or blog creates trust with Google.

How To Write Compelling Content

As you know by now, SEO is becoming more competitive than ever before. The engineers at Google will continue to do everything they can to stick it to marketing companies who try to game the system. (And rightfully so.)

The kind of SEO that works from a long-term prospect is the content that achieves the objectives of your readers, educating them and using social media and other channels to push that content out.

You should focus on enhancing the natural authority of websites, pages which creates industry influence and trust with Google.

You have to remember that Google is on the side of the people using their search engine. They don't care two hoots about you or your product. You are not their customer. The people using Goolge are the ones who they are making money off of.

Smart content marketers derive benefit from audience-focused content and by social media exposure and sharing. This enables you to build a profitable audience that is an asset even if your search engine rankings disappear.

Social media traffic is crucial because it allows you to develop more long-term traffic sources like email subscribers and higher search engine rankings. But unfortunately, this is not a quick fix.

People who are searching for something specific are in a very different mood and frame of mind then when they are socializing on Facebook. Of course, it depends on the product but people don't go on Facebook to shop. (Although that's changing with Facebook Marketplace.) That's why Facebook advertising can be difficult because you have to interrupt their patterns to get them to take action. Remember, always think about the mindset of the viewer!

On Google Bots

Google determines search engine optimization by what is known as crawling. These Google bots are like those machines in the Matrix that go around searching for humans. These bits of computer code information on the web and continue onto the different links from your page to other pages.

These bots periodically return looking for change to the original page which means they are always opportunities to modify the way a search engine sees and evaluates your content down the road. If for any reason the spider can't see your content or doesn't understand what it's about your page can't be indexed and ranked.

The bots do not just casually analyse the content but also stores it in a giant database. This is called indexing. The bots' role is to save every bit of your content it crawls for the future benefit of its searchers. Indexing is, of course, the critical aspect for SEO writers to crack and this is a jealously guarded algorithm by Google. This is in layman terms saying that Google has a complex set of rules in which they determine where your content and webpage show up.

Search engines have come a long way since the early days of the web. You can no longer fool them with content farming and poor-quality websites that try to game the system and don't actually serve a purpose.

Chapter Eleven:

Copywriting in the New Century

How vain it is to sit down to write when you have not stood up to live."

– Henry David Thoreau

Copywriting has undergone many significant changes since the 1920s when mass advertising came into its own, and copywriting, as a profession, started to become extremely important. In the 1950s, TV, print, and radio advertising budgets were beginning to skyrocket and the trend for large multinational corporations to spend millions, if not billions on advertising continued for the rest of the 20th century.

In early 2000, a lot of that money shifted towards digital marketing. Now we will continue to see digital marketing expand and become even more competitive. Search engine optimization, content marketing, and pay-per-click ads are expected to be the largest portion of spending.

Marketing has been revolutionized by the internet and copywriters are going to have to be very savvy and nimble when it comes to embracing the new changes on the horizon.

We live in an age where people's attention spans are now measured in seconds rather than minutes. Online copy is not so much read as scanned. Video is becoming cheaper and easily accessible on your tablet or mobile phones. And it's compressed; look at how news, ideas and opinions are shoe-horned into 140 characters or less on Twitter. Does it really take a copywriter to craft a bullet point or tweet that someone will devour in seconds?

Offline ads, printed media, and mailers (as they used to be called) will soon all but disappear. Newspapers and magazines face shrinking readerships. It's increasingly hard to reach a national audience.

I'm not saying this just to be provocative. I mean look around you – we live in an age where people's attention spans are now measured in seconds rather than minutes. We have so many options; with a click of a button, we can do or get almost anything we want. We have many messages constantly battling for our attention. Online copy is not so much read as scanned. And it's compressed; look at how news, ideas and opinions are squished into pictures, alerts, and on Twitter into140 characters. Does it really take a copywriter to craft a bullet point or tweet that someone will devour in seconds?

Another characteristic of online content is its exponential growth. Search engines such as Google are responsible for much of this increase. Many businesses create content with the primary goal of appearing high in the search results. Although this is changing as Google algorithms get smarter, the volume of copy often takes precedence over quality. Why pay a professional copywriter when you can find someone in India or the Philippines to churn out a page of text with your keywords in it for just a few pennies.

Just as technology can create content it is also responsible for reducing it. Devices such as the Apple Watch and other 'wearables' with small screens means that space for words is at a premium. Copy for display on such devices will by necessity have to be stripped down to its basics.

But why write anything at all when there is video? This is a fast-growing medium – among younger age-groups in particular. YouTube is now the world's second-largest search engine as people seek information in a visual format. Advertisers have been quick to seize the opportunity that video presents. New formats such as 6-second long Vines and Instagram videos are more and more popular. Could this spell the end of the written word?

Of course not, because today everyone is a copywriter. Anyone can write pretty much anything and publish it online. Tweet, blog post, product review, comment – the opportunities are endless. But if everyone can do it, where does that leave the art of copywriting? Does it have a future? Is there even a need for it anymore?

There is just as much skill in copywriting a tweet as a long-form landing page, a press ad or a glossy brochure. It's about knowing the words that persuade or influence. And it's about knowing what to leave in and what to leave out. Good copywriting makes readers click the link in a tweet. It encourages them to read right to the end of a long-form landing page and sign up for the offer. It entices people to call the number in the press ad or pop into their local retail outlet. And it makes the reader desire the item in the glossy brochure.

The copywriter's craft isn't limited to visible words on a page or device screen, however. It applies just as much to video too. It takes good copywriting to make a video that is persuasive. With just about anyone with a smartphone able to make a video, copywriting often gets overlooked. However, it shouldn't. Not by a long shot.

Content marketing and social media are set to continue to flood the internet with words. Most of them will be at best mediocre. Good copywriting and good content, thanks to Google's focus on quality, will float to the top and gain in prominence and value. You need to improve your craft. Be the best. There is no other way to compete with this mediocracy.

Machines will get smarter and machine-generated text will improve. If anything, this will increase the demand for copy written by a skilled human copywriter. That's because companies will demand content that stands out from their competitors. Will machines ever able to write copy like Apples' "Think Different" or DeBeers "A Diamond Is Forever" ads? They are only a couple of words each but they communicate so much. A computer won't be able to encompass an entire brand's identity in two words, or transform an entire industry.

Globalization is sure to increase over the next decade but audiences will become ever more fragmented. Marketing to the individual will grow in importance and persuasive personalized messages will be the key. Instead of 'dumbed down' copy, web visitors will expect dynamic pages with copy tailored to their needs and interests – wherever they are in the world.

Moreover, globalization means that a copywriter's market is global too. It will be easier than ever to get business from the other side of the planet. The flipside of this is, of course, that there'll be more competition but what's life without a challenge or two!

We're living in an era when anyone can write 'copy' with no training and little effort. Soon machines will be able to do so too. Yet the craft of copywriting is not dying. Instead, the opportunities are greater than ever before. Why? Because copywriting is a craft that produces words that persuade and influence – not ones that just fill a tweet or a page. And there'll always be a demand for that.

www.ingramcontent.com/pod-product-compliance
Lightning Source LLC
Chambersburg PA
CBHW050908260726

48660CB00001B/96